Food Art: Art + Tech

~~~~~~~

This is the first edition of **"Food Art: Art + Tech"**.

The concept of this artbook is inspired in the fusion of different traditional art techniques and innovatives techniques using Artificial Intelligence (Ai), neural networks, digital designs.

- One day, someone asked me - Why "Food Art"?-

My answer comes from my heart: - Because food, art and technology are my real passions in life. I have joined them in this project for everybody who enjoy life, nature, art and all the life's pleasures that are closed to us.

I was inspired to paint these artworks by my beloved partner in life, who is my shiny moon everyday.

All of the pictures showned in this book are artworks made by the author and artist Silvia Fernandez Romay with the collaboration of Atelier Digital & AlphotoArt.

I hope you enjoy this book as well as I enjoy it doing it.

~~~~~~~

Art + Technology

is the present right now

Artist – Author : Silvia Fernandez Romay

Collaboration partners: Atelier Digital & AlphotoArt

All rights reserved. Copyright © - Silvia Fernandez Romay - 2022 -

~~~~~

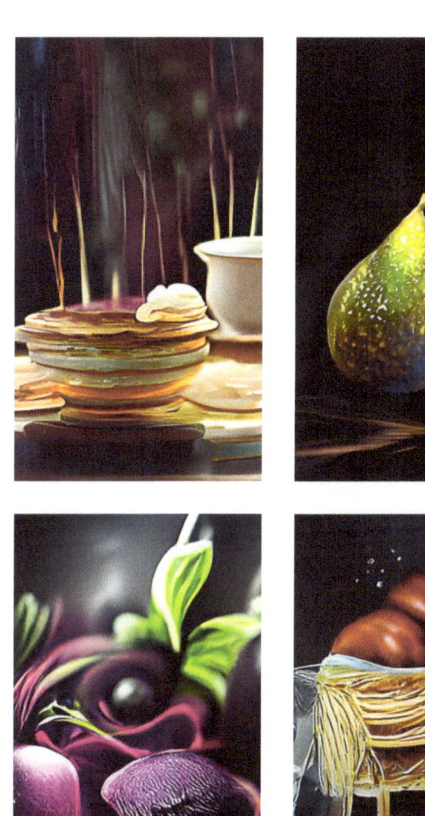
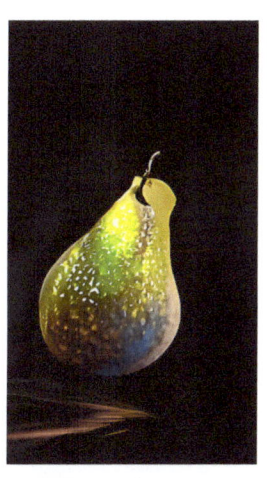
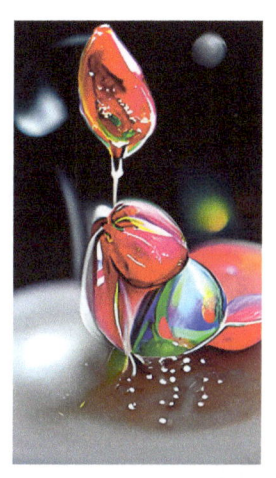
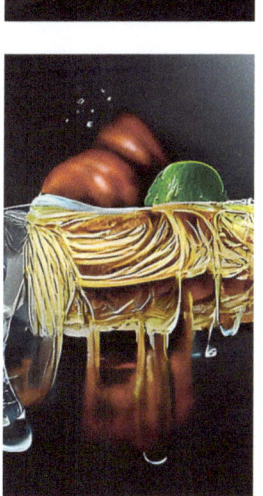
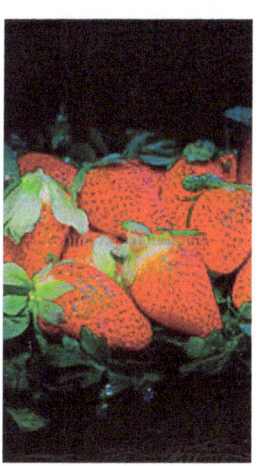

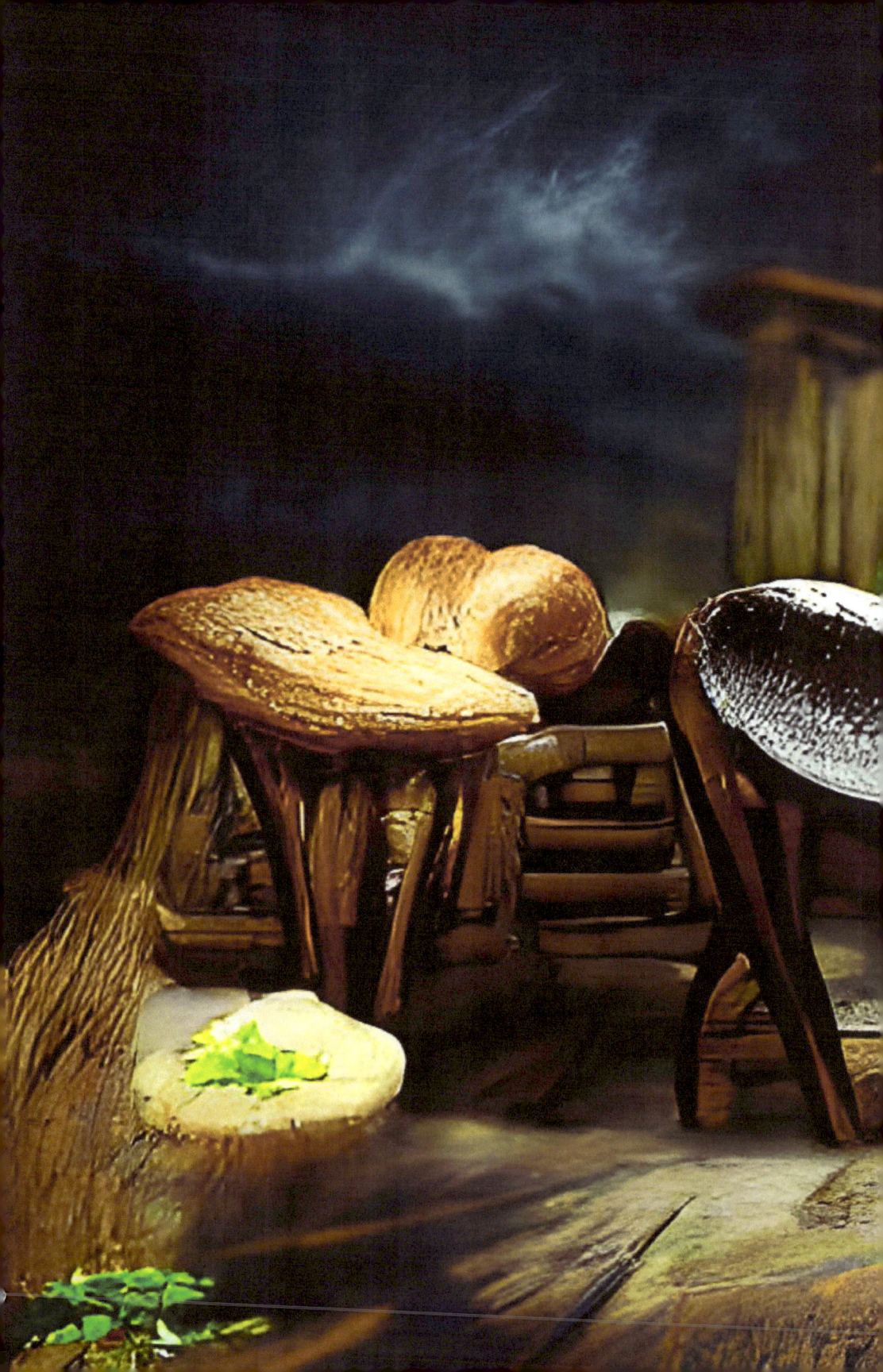

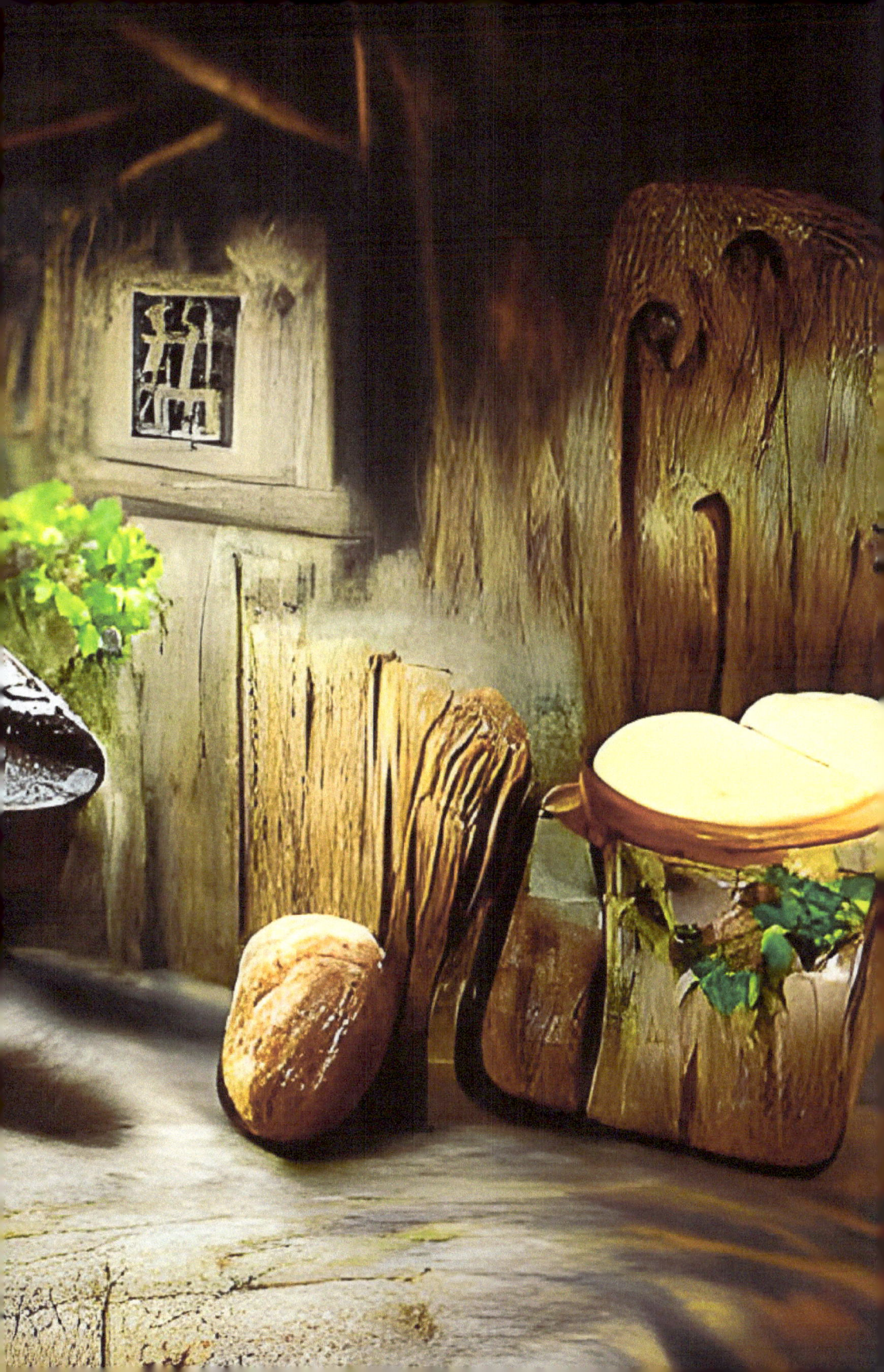

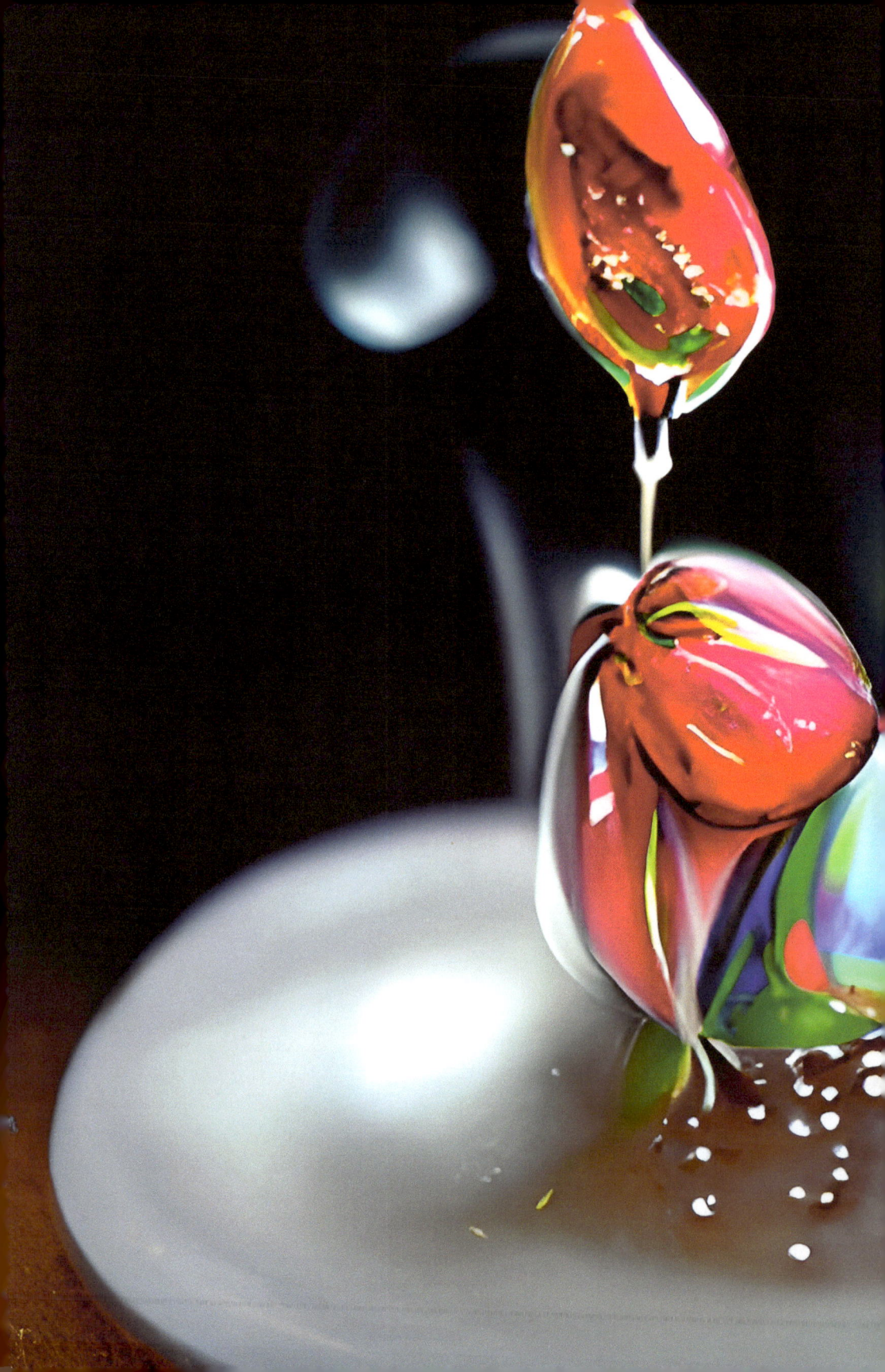

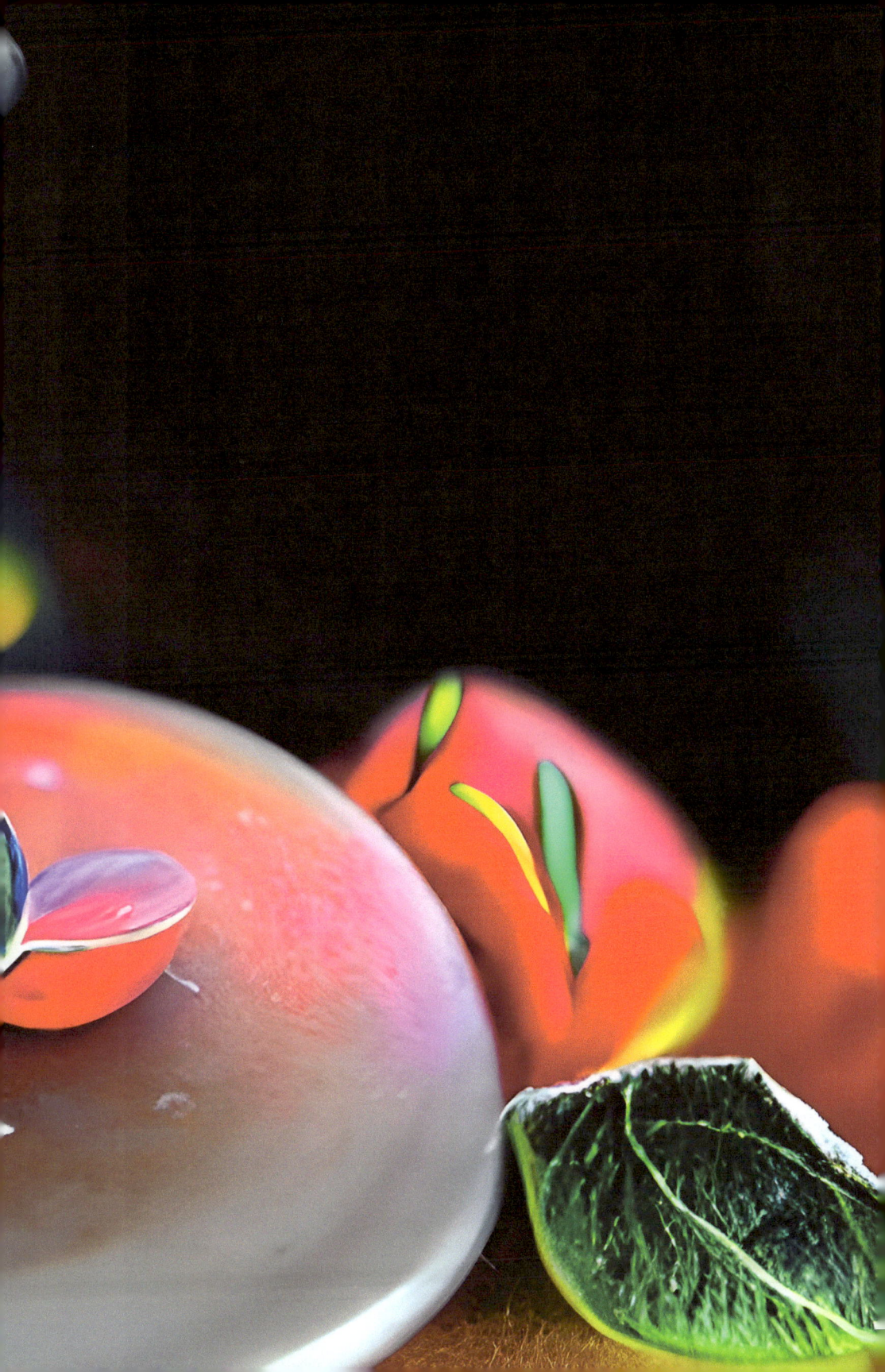

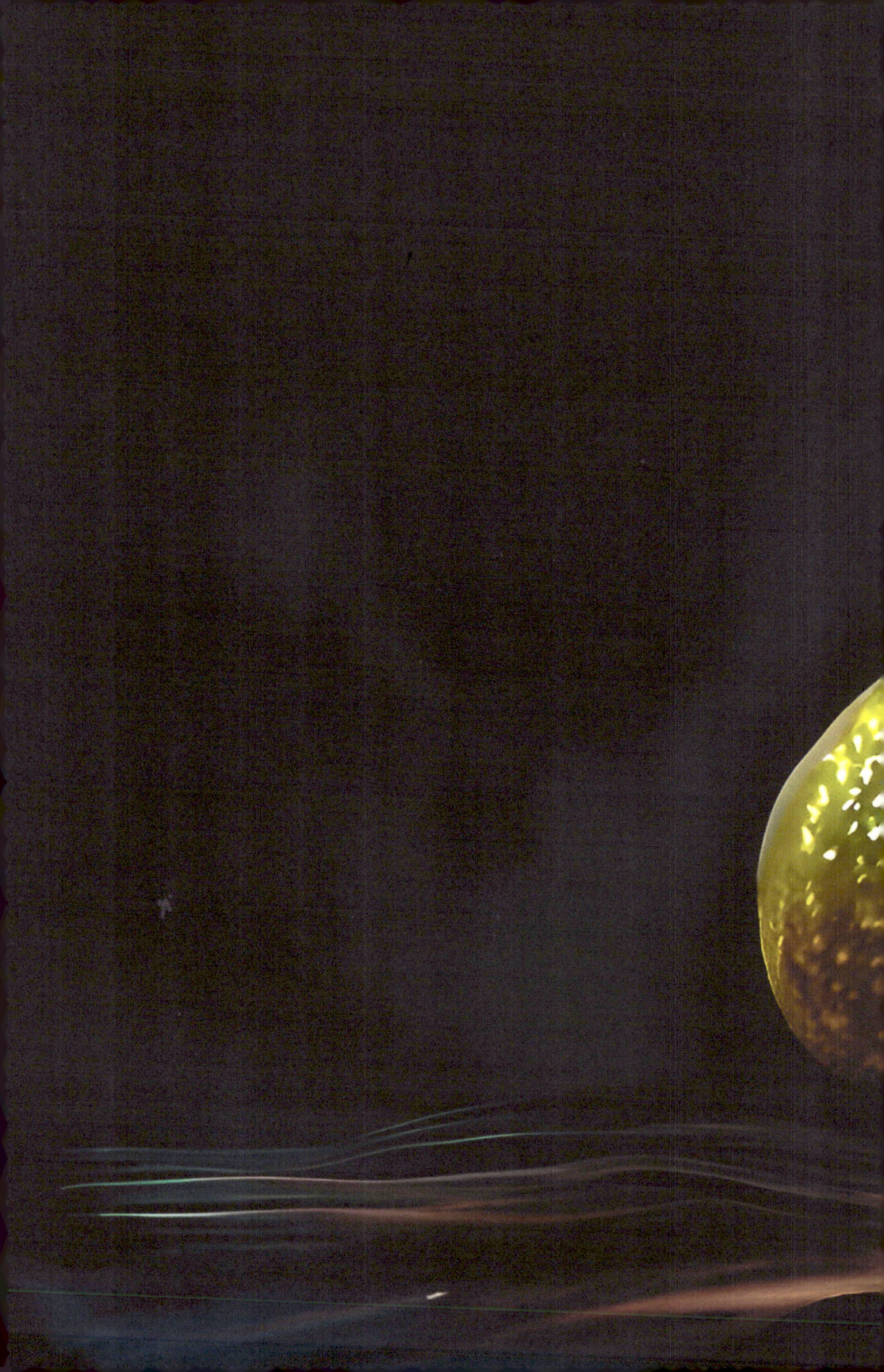

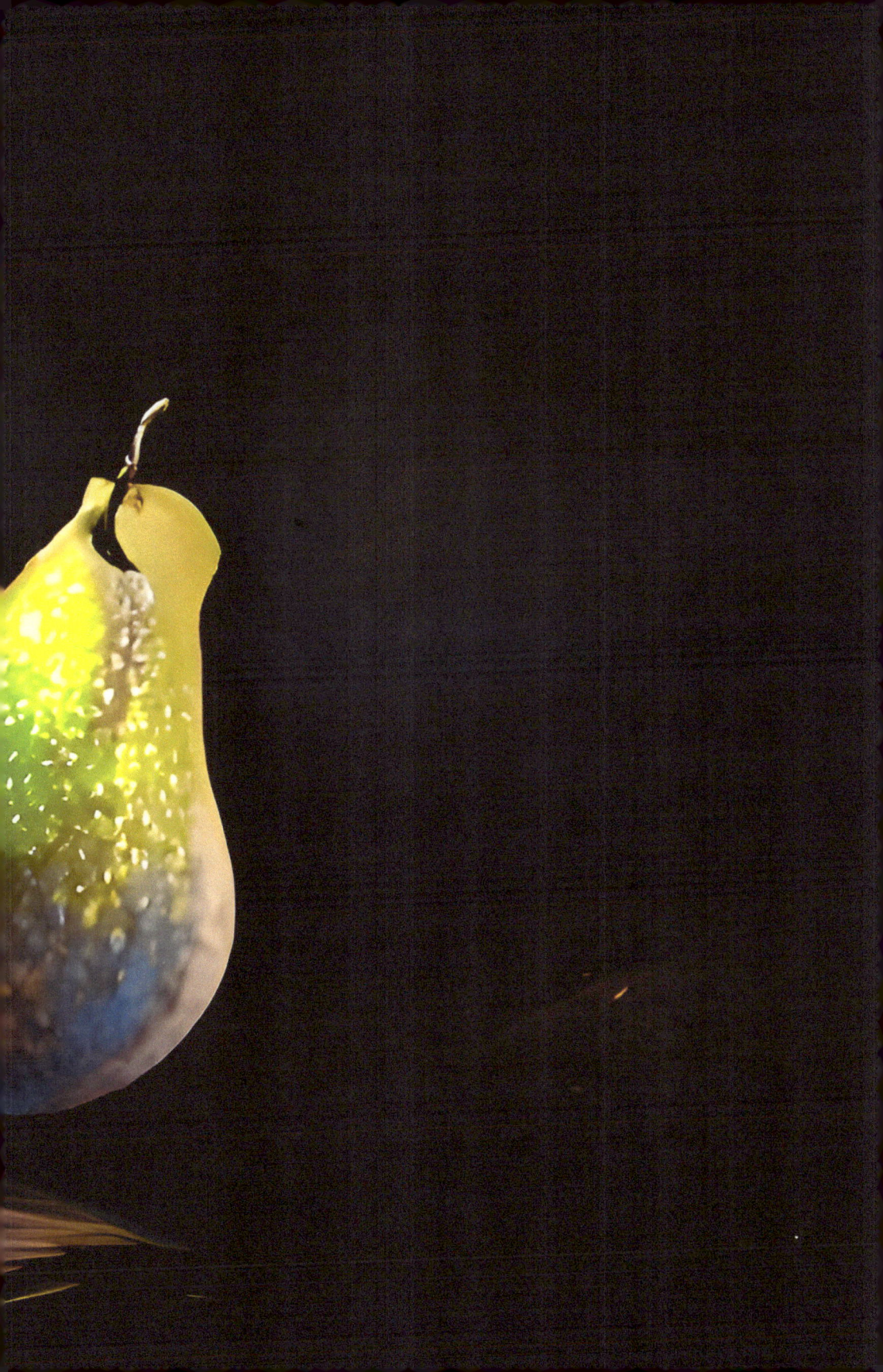

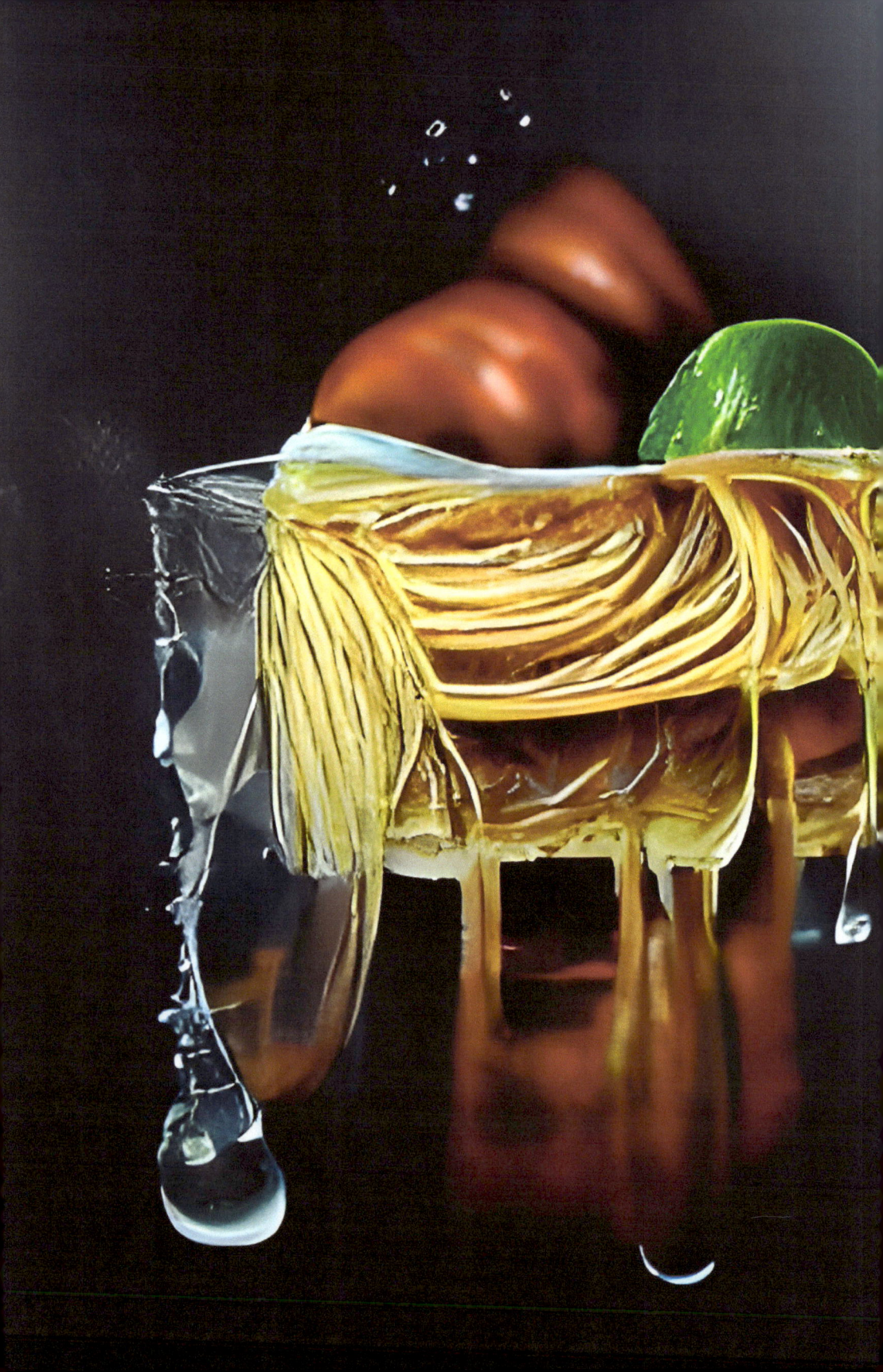

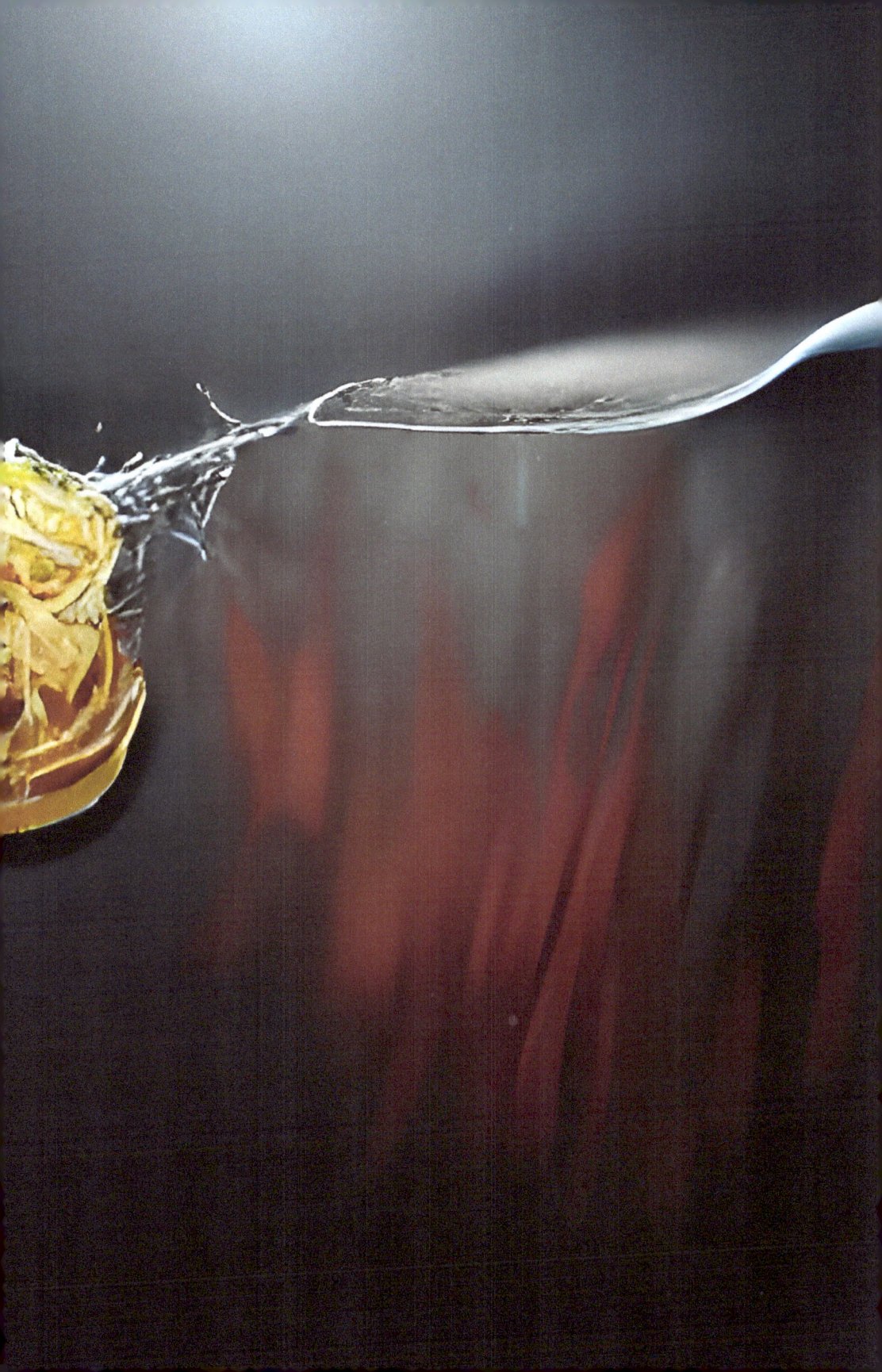

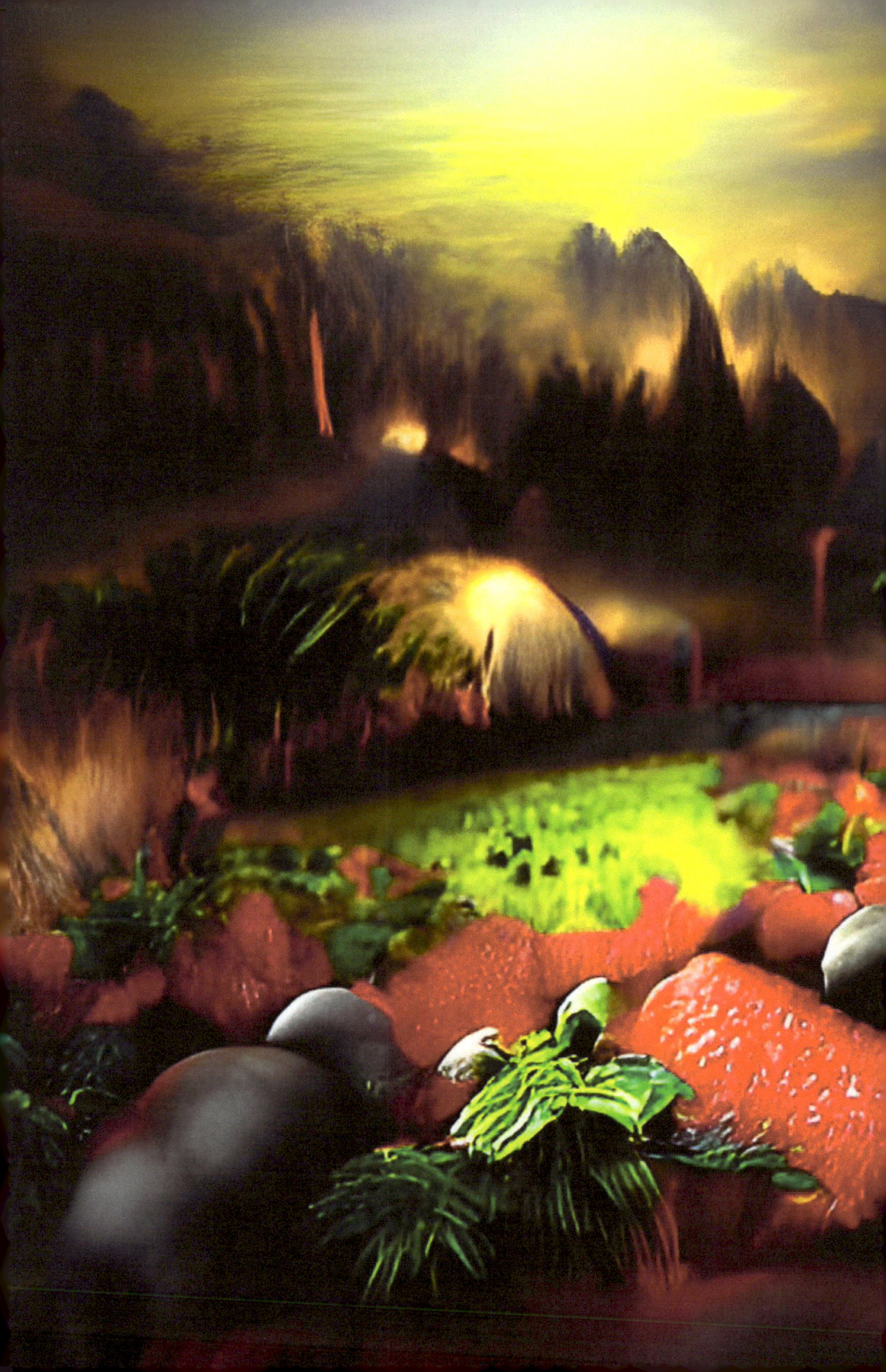

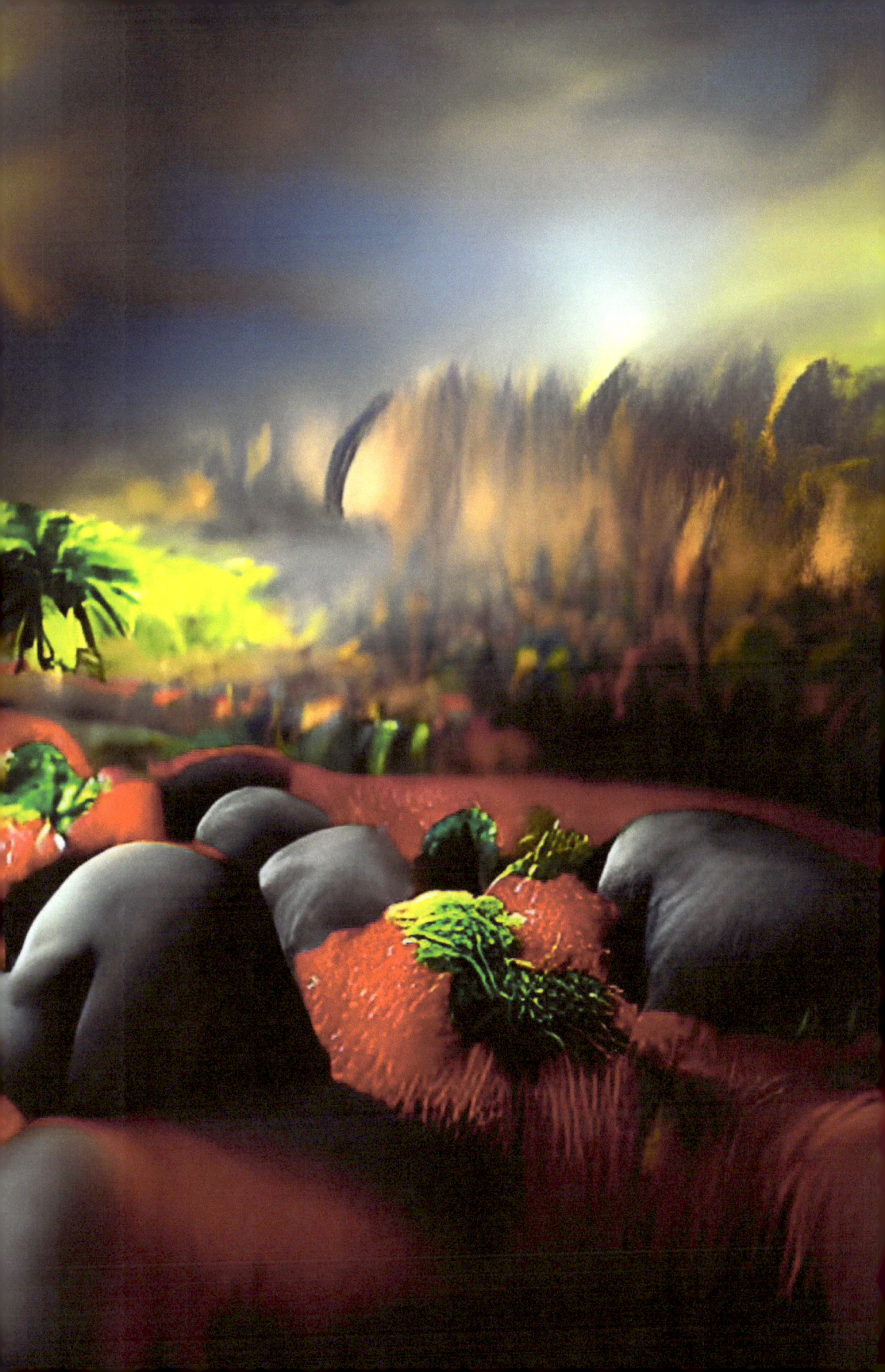

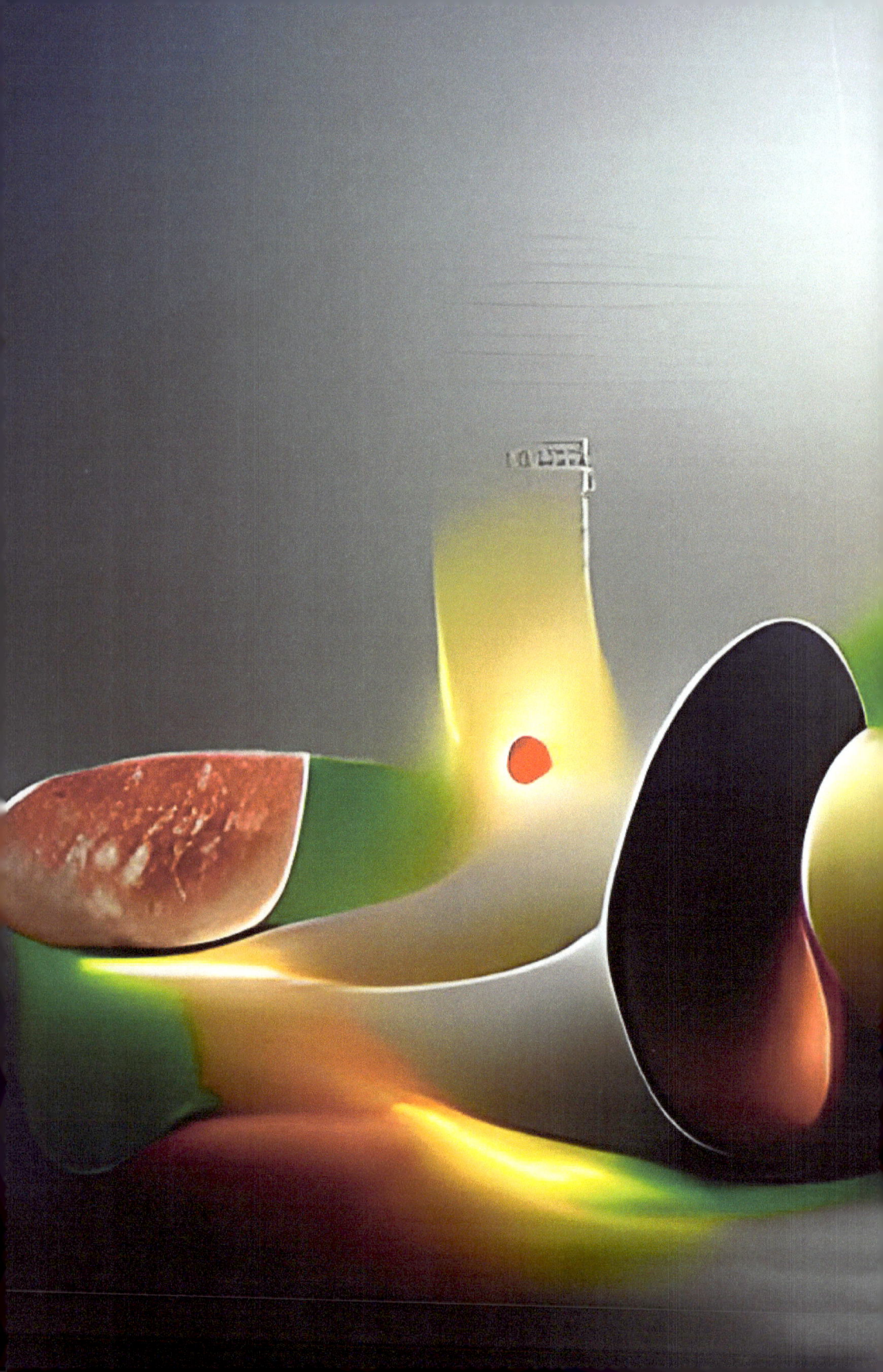

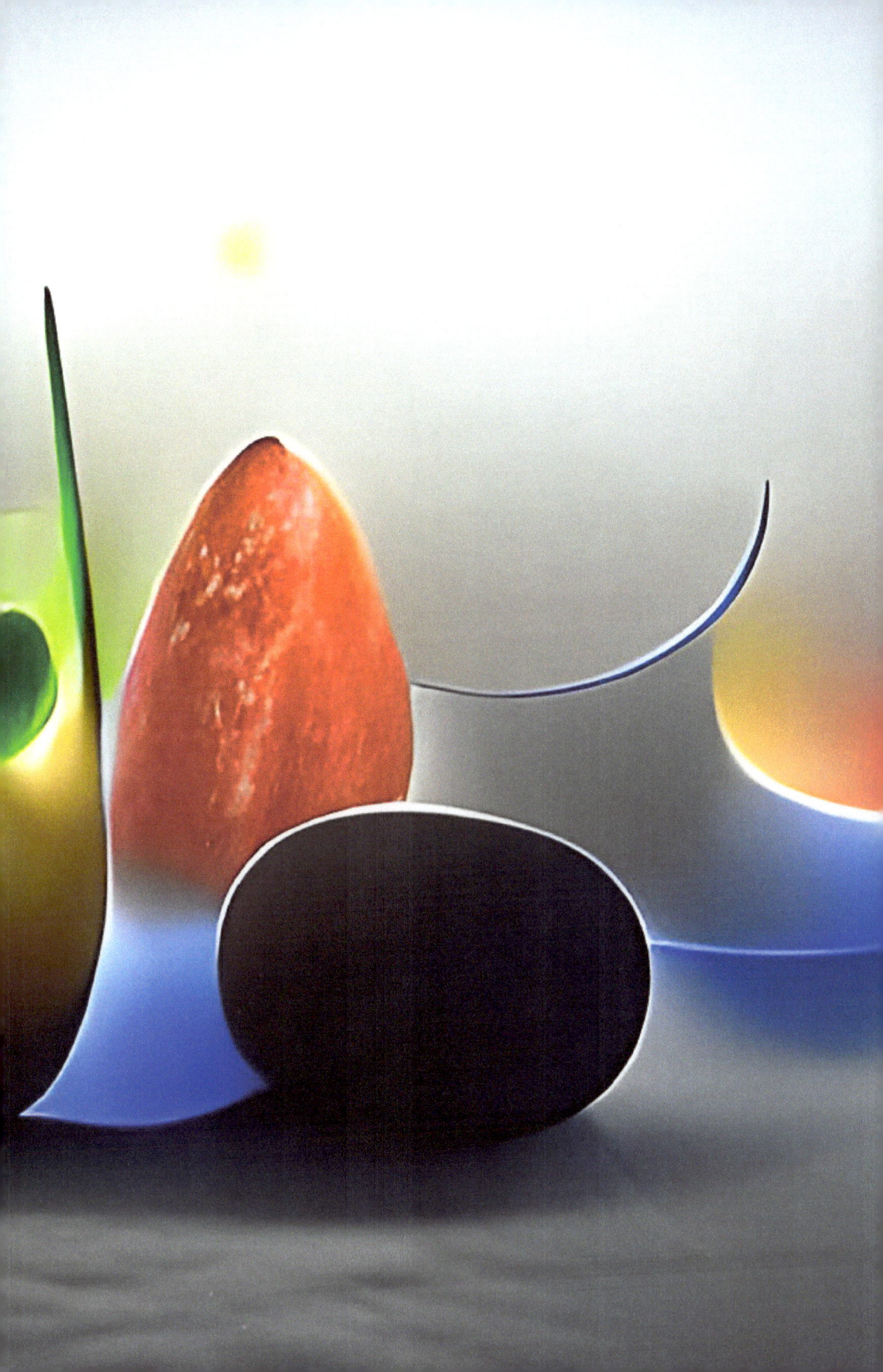

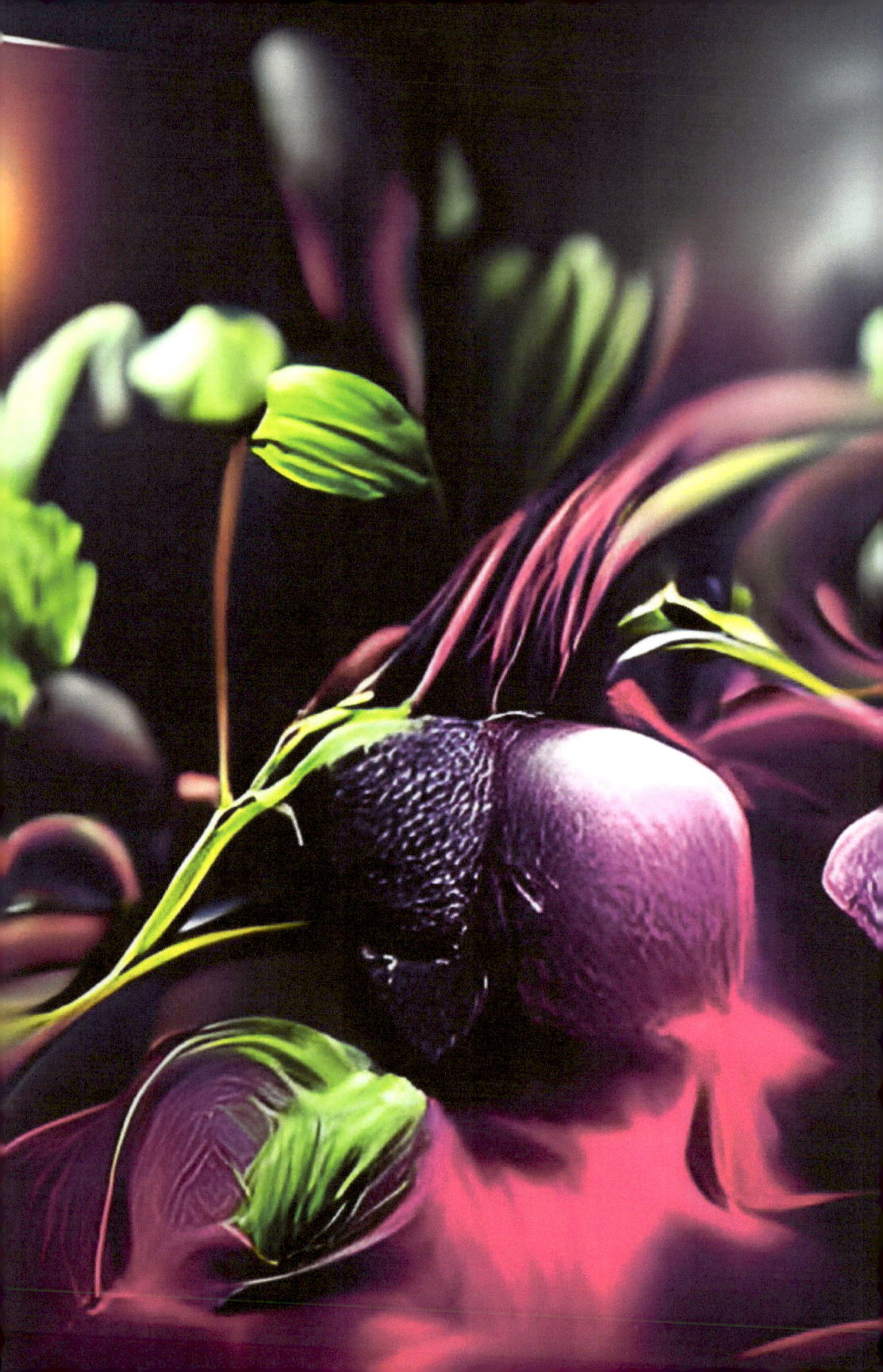

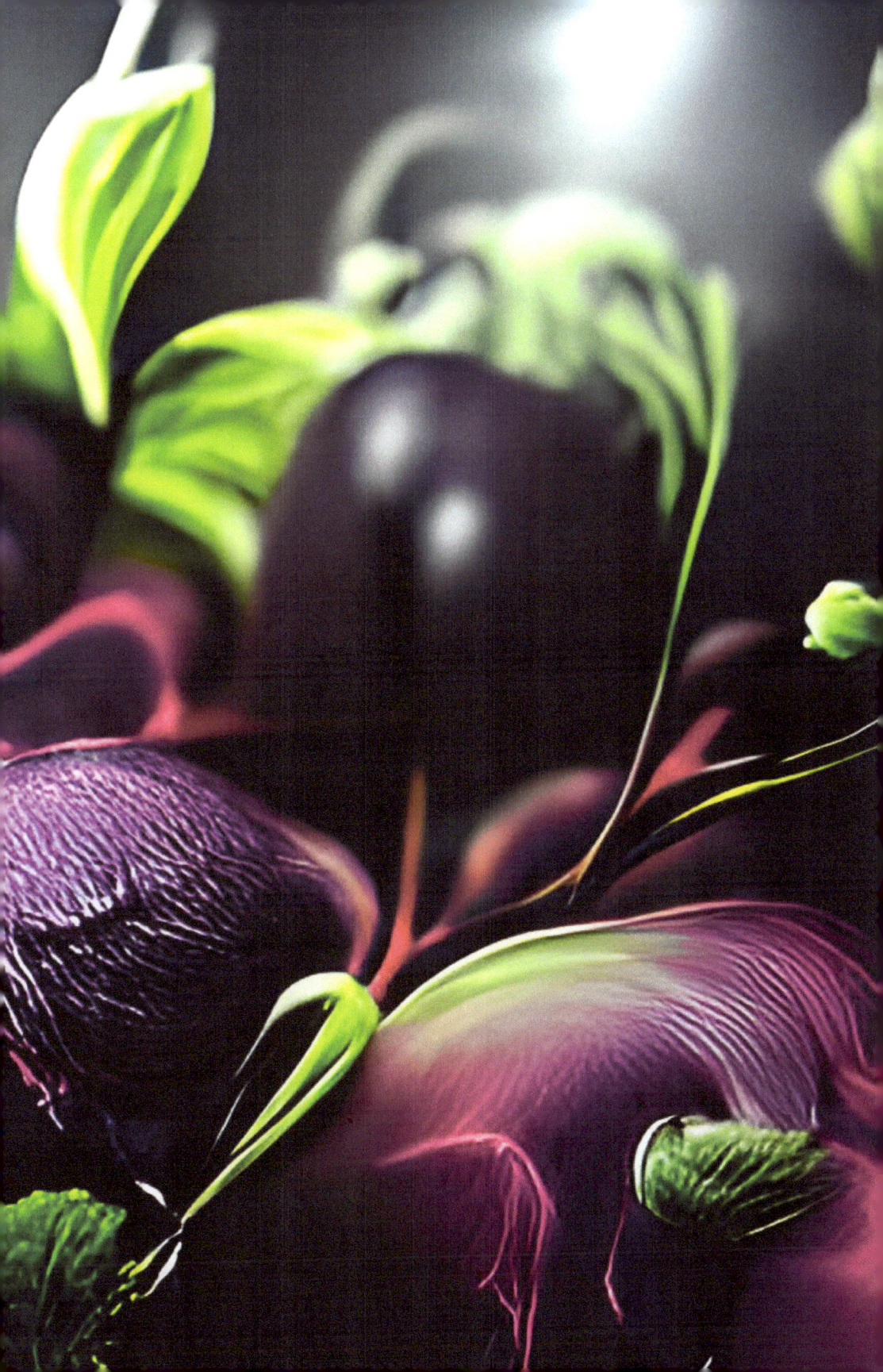

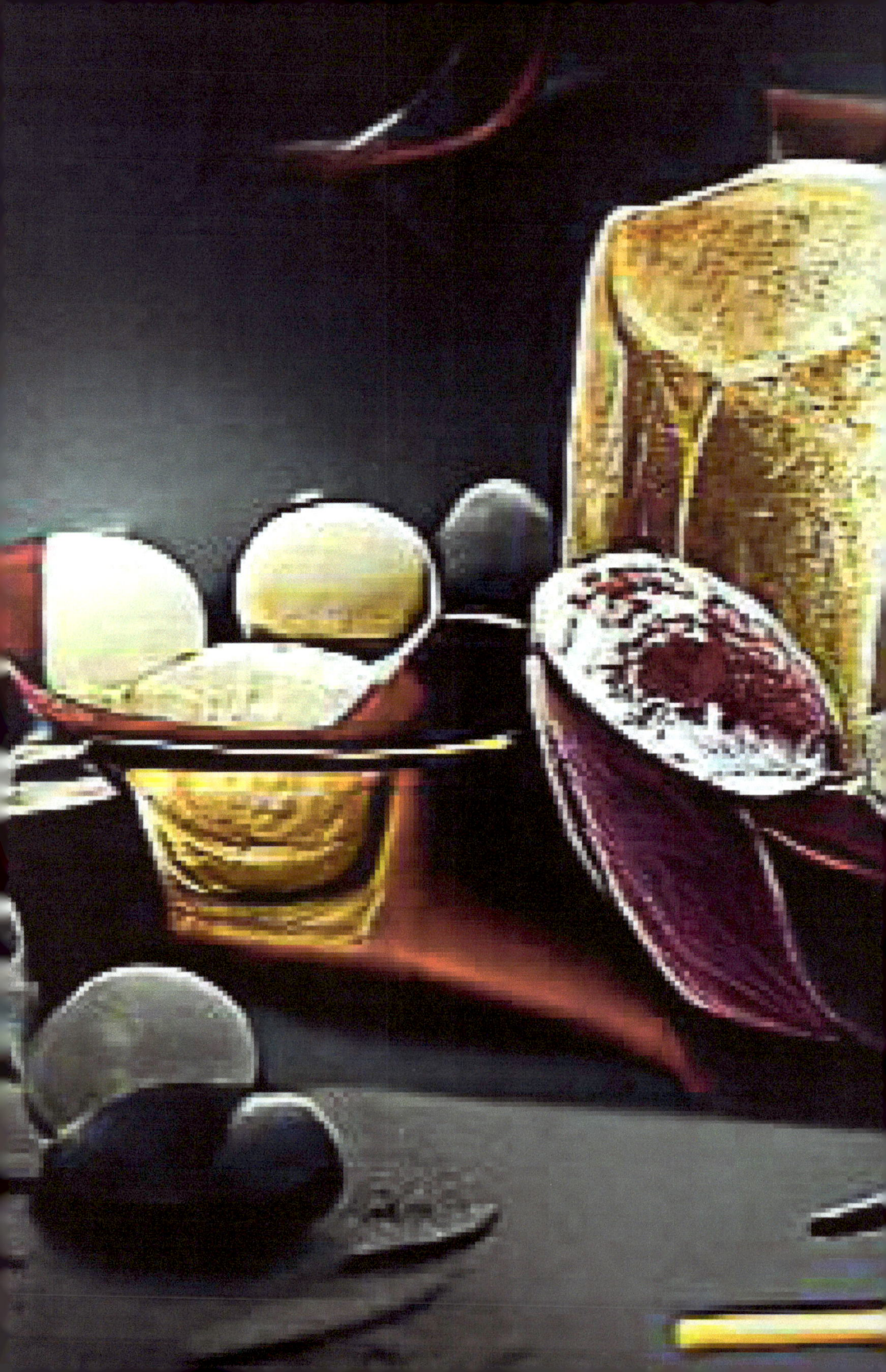

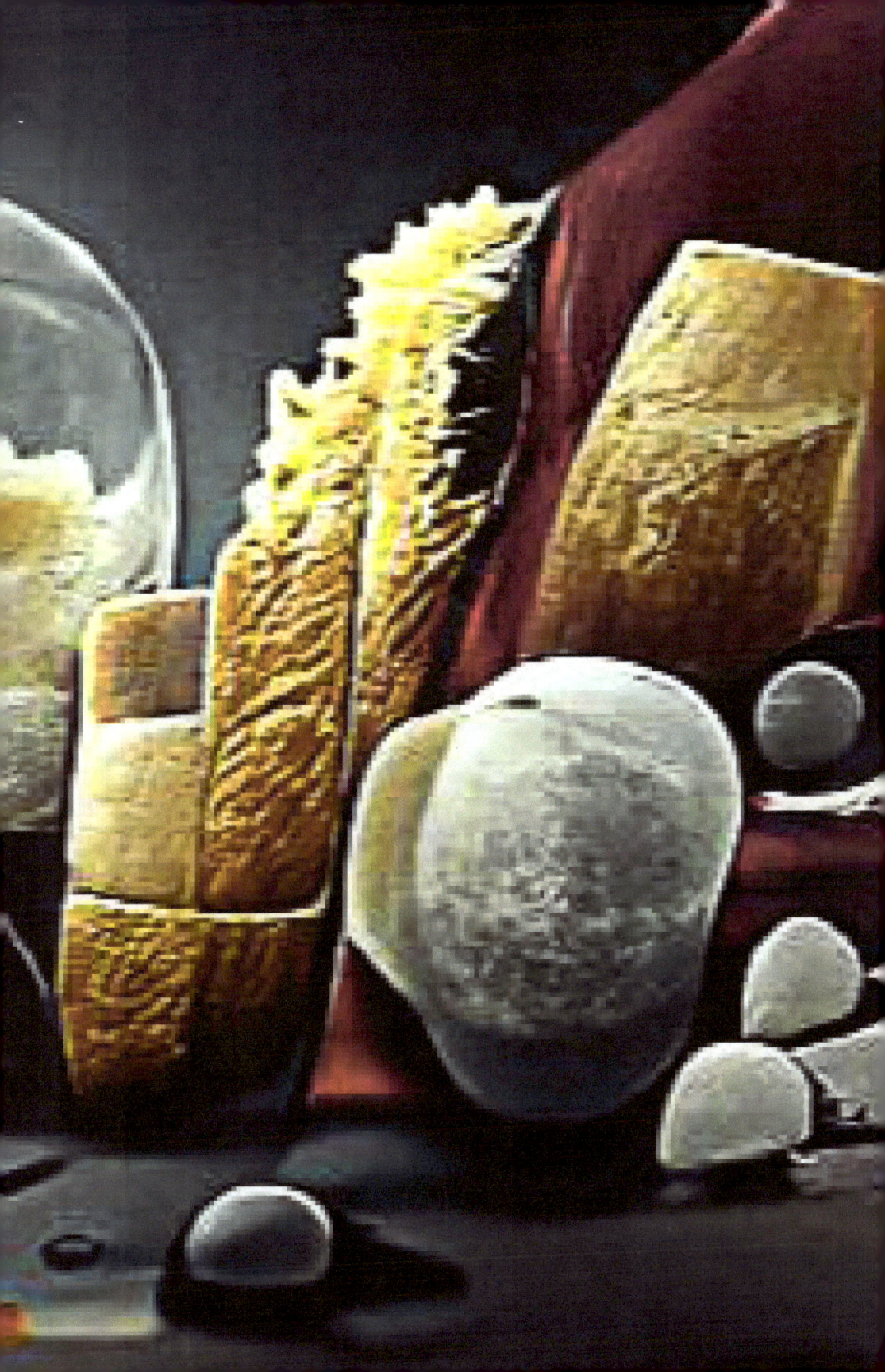

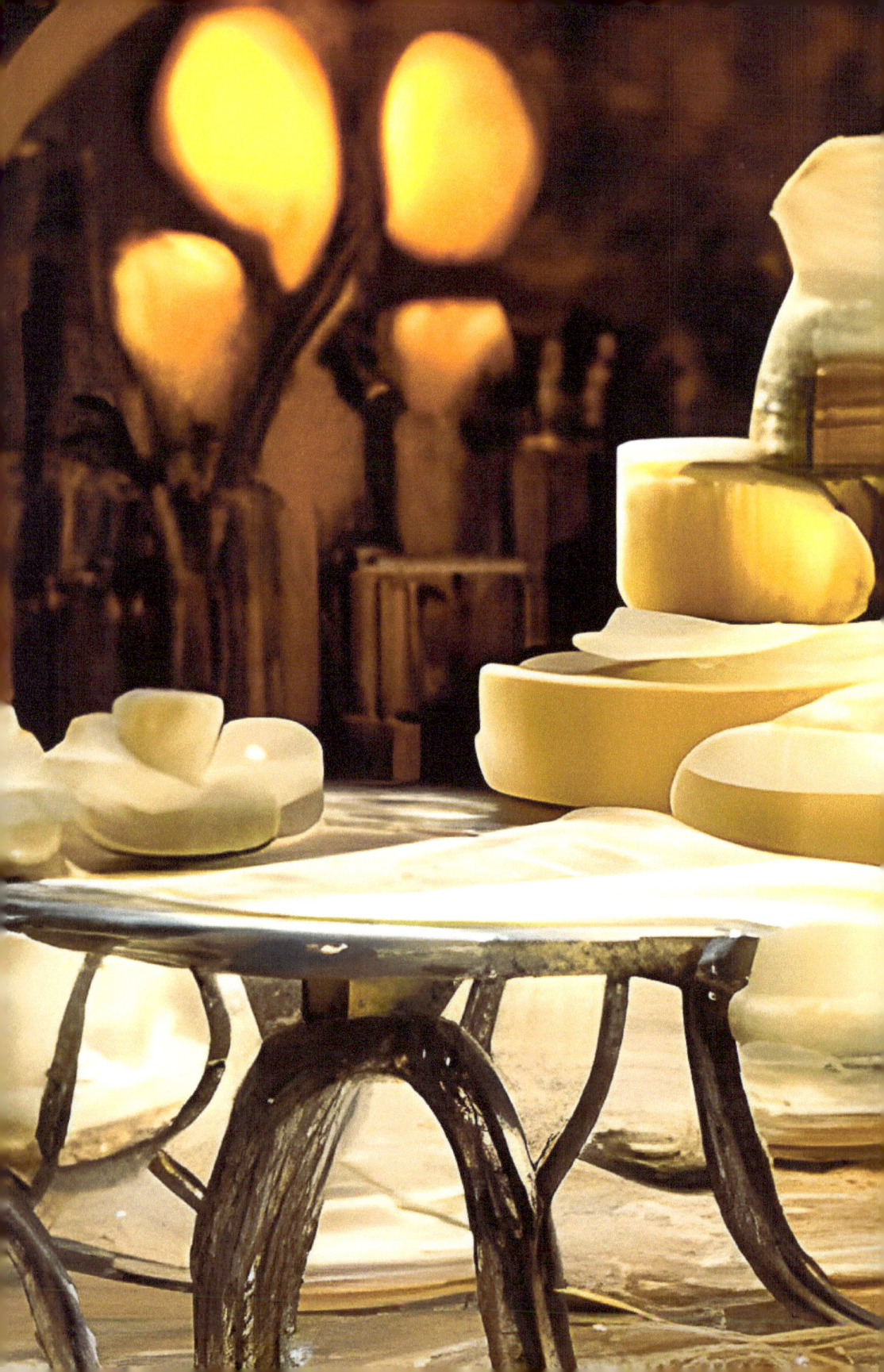

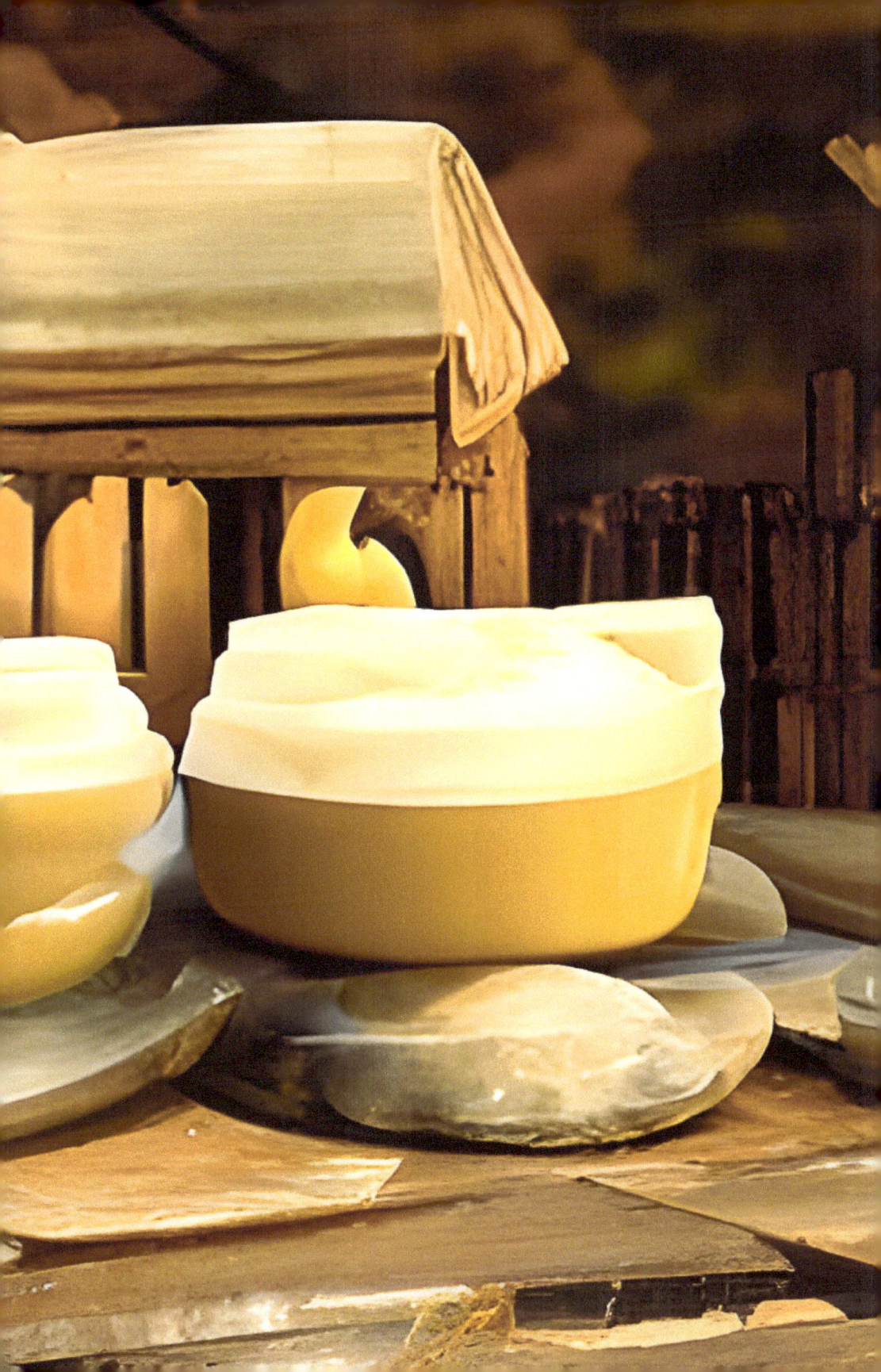

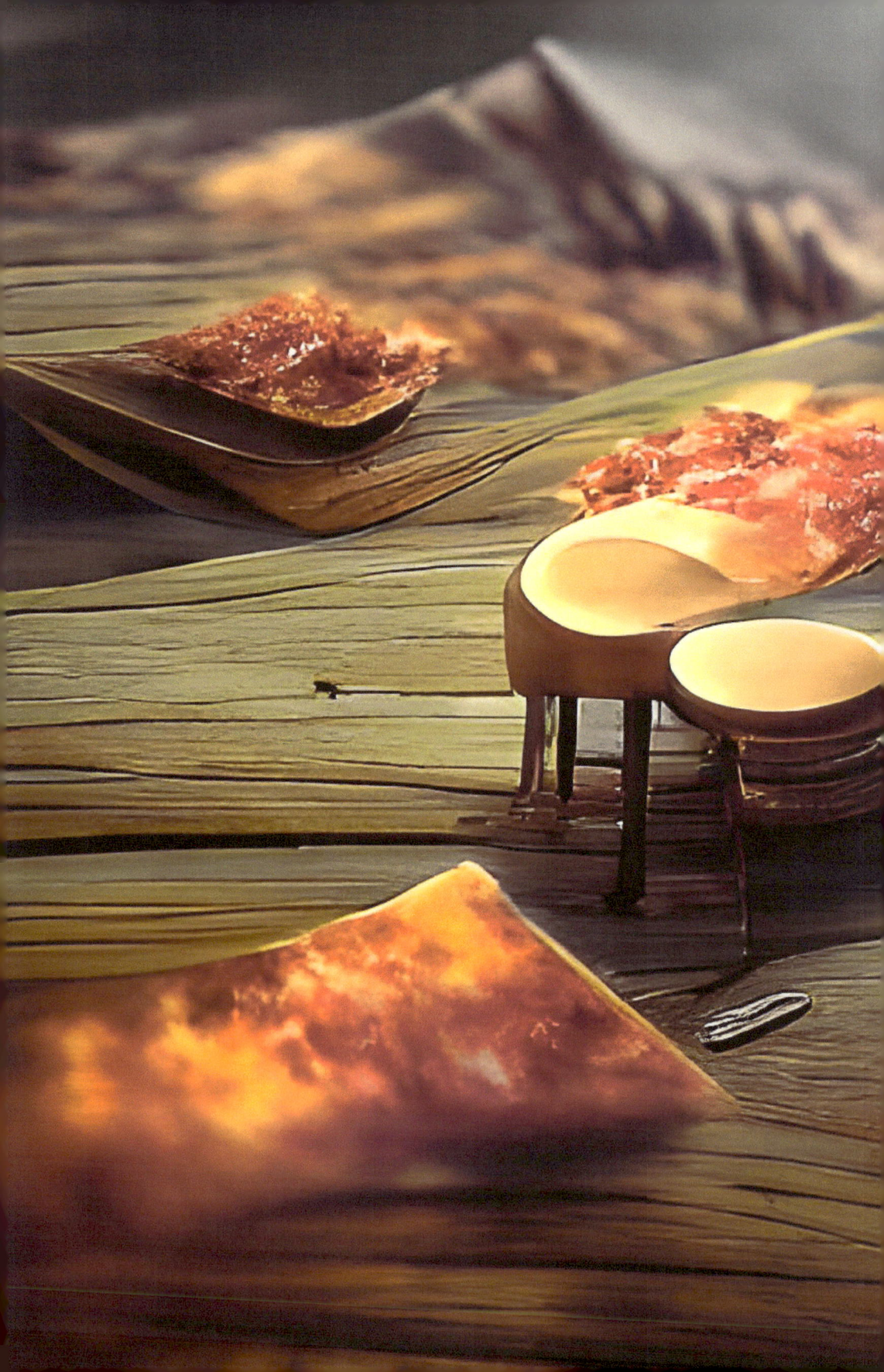

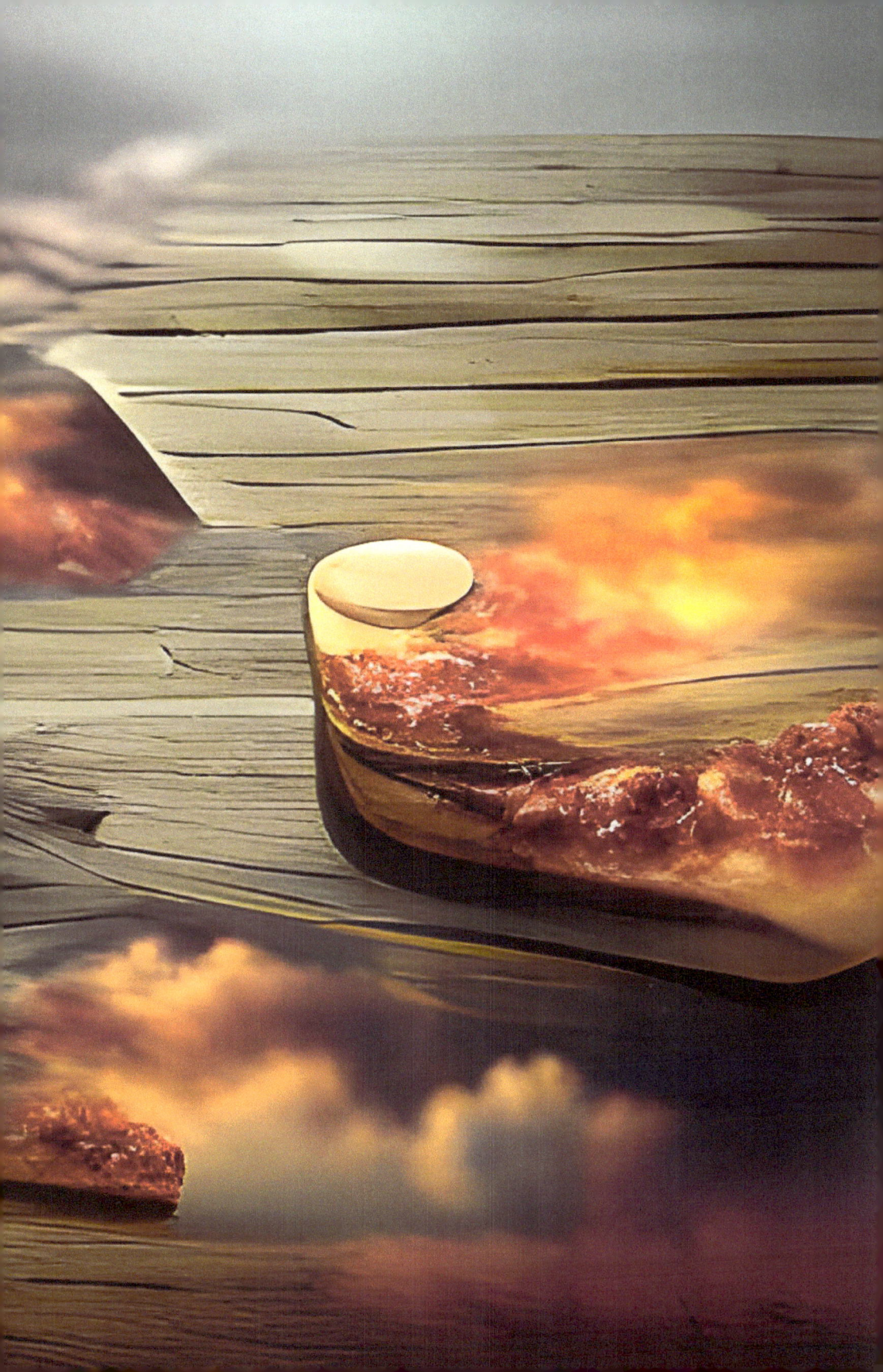

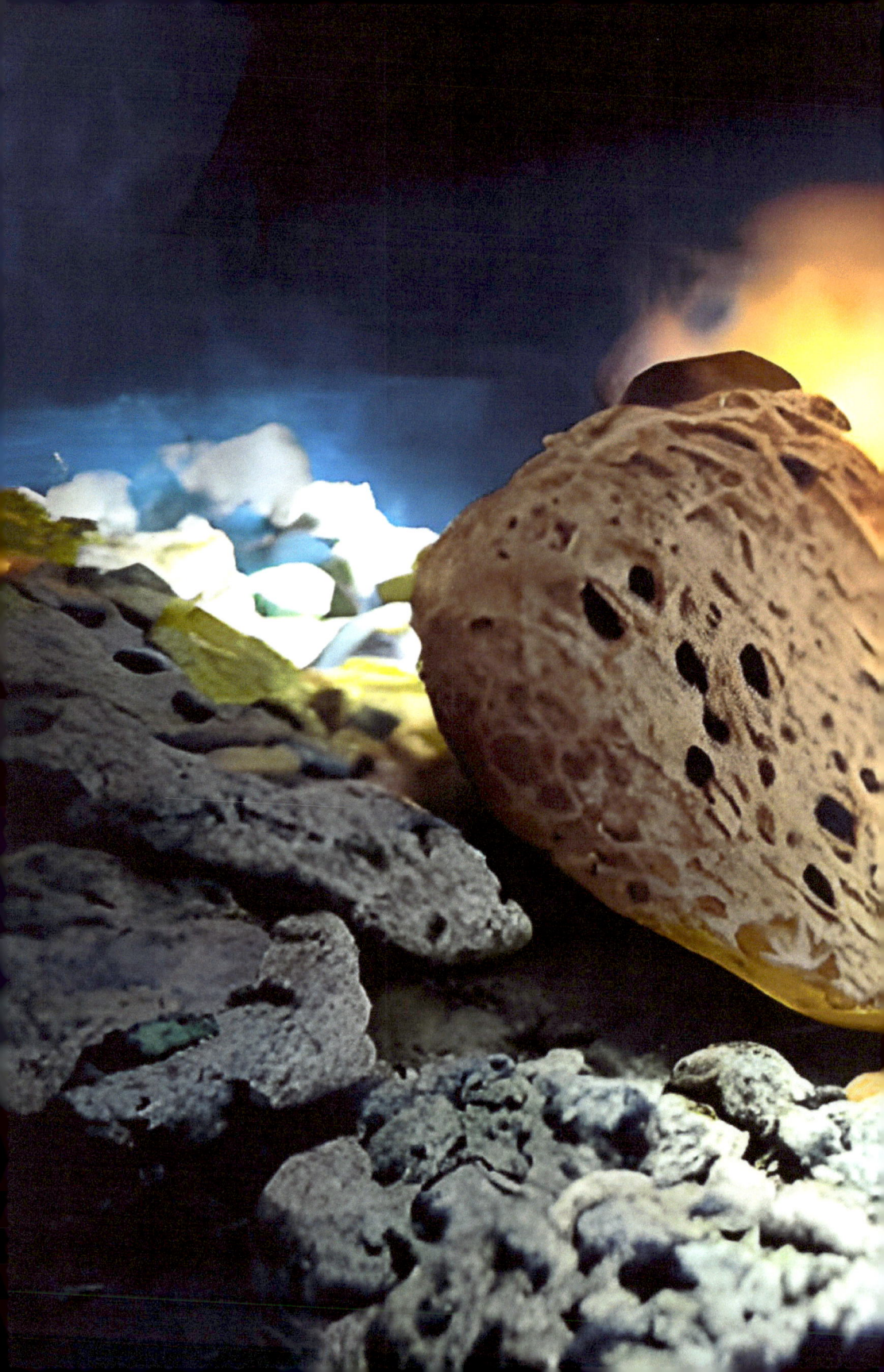

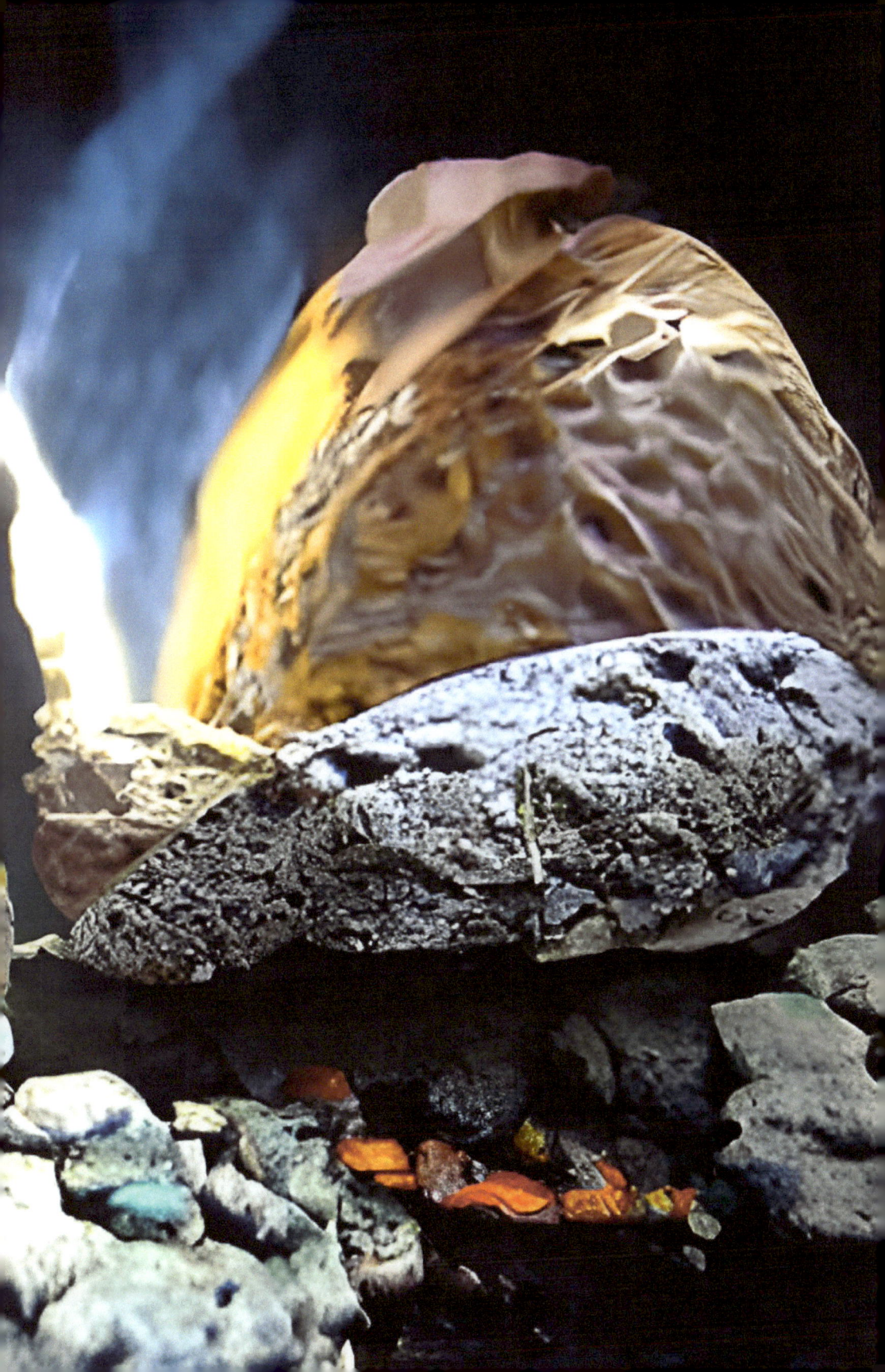

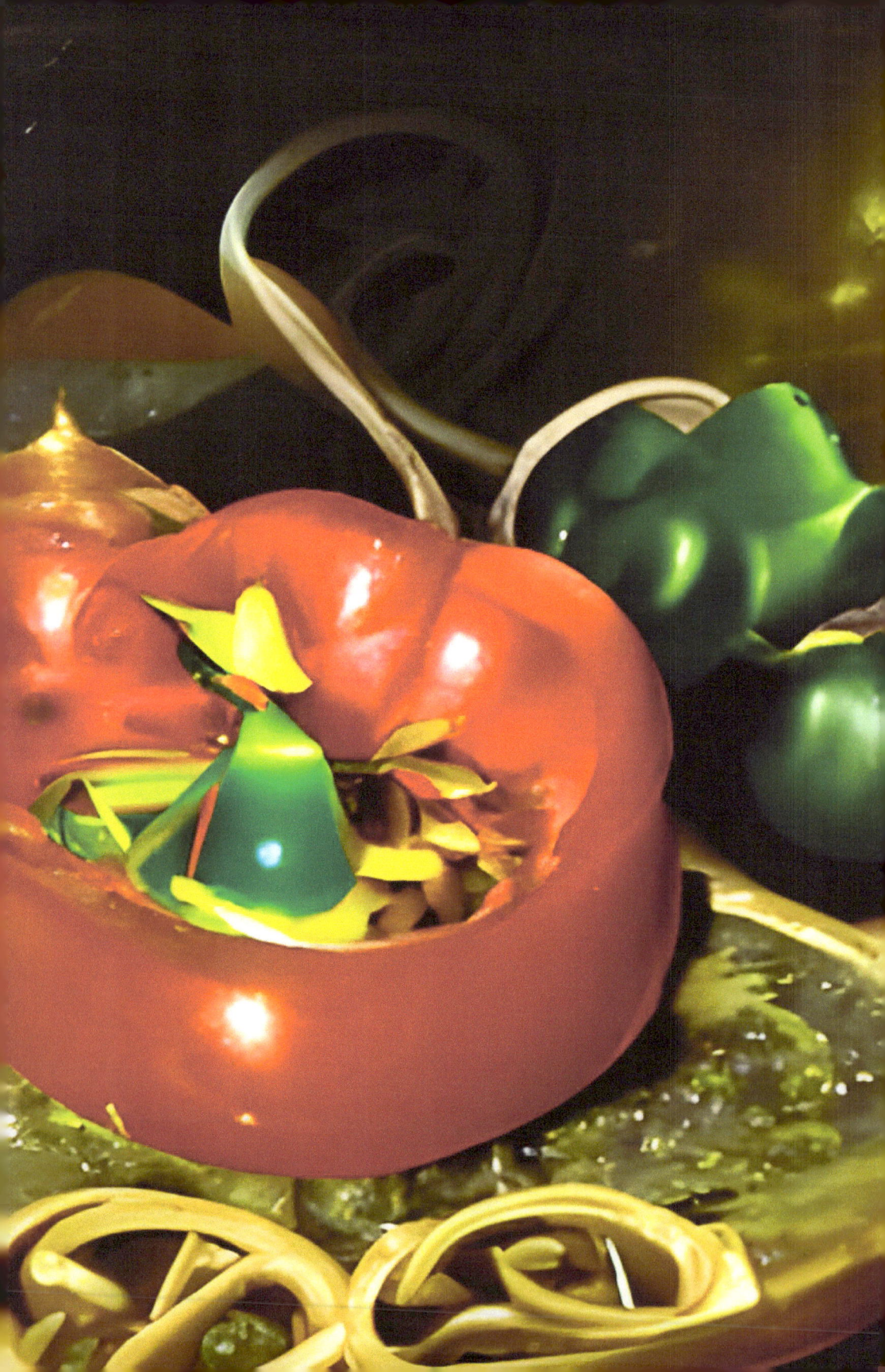

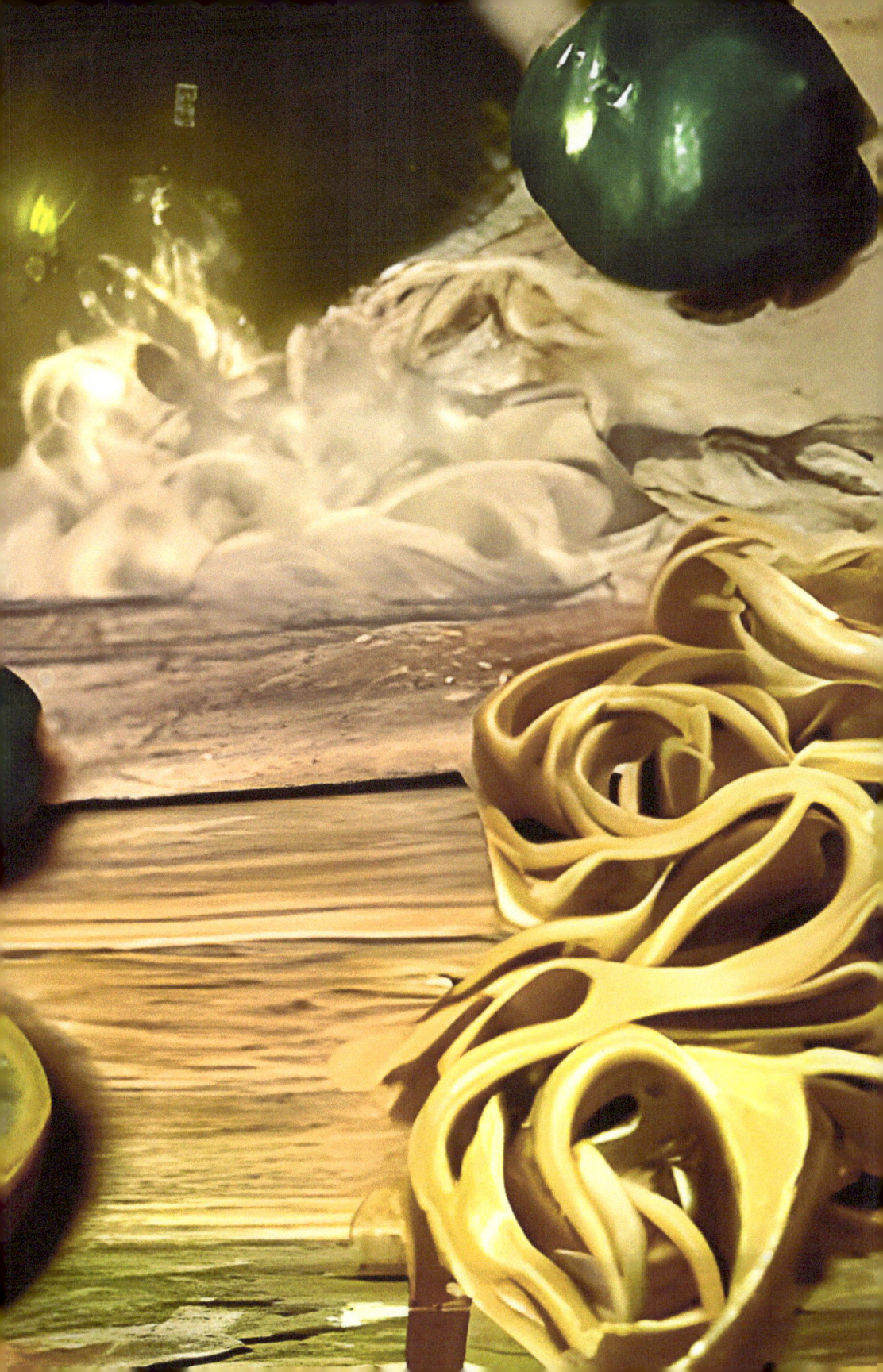

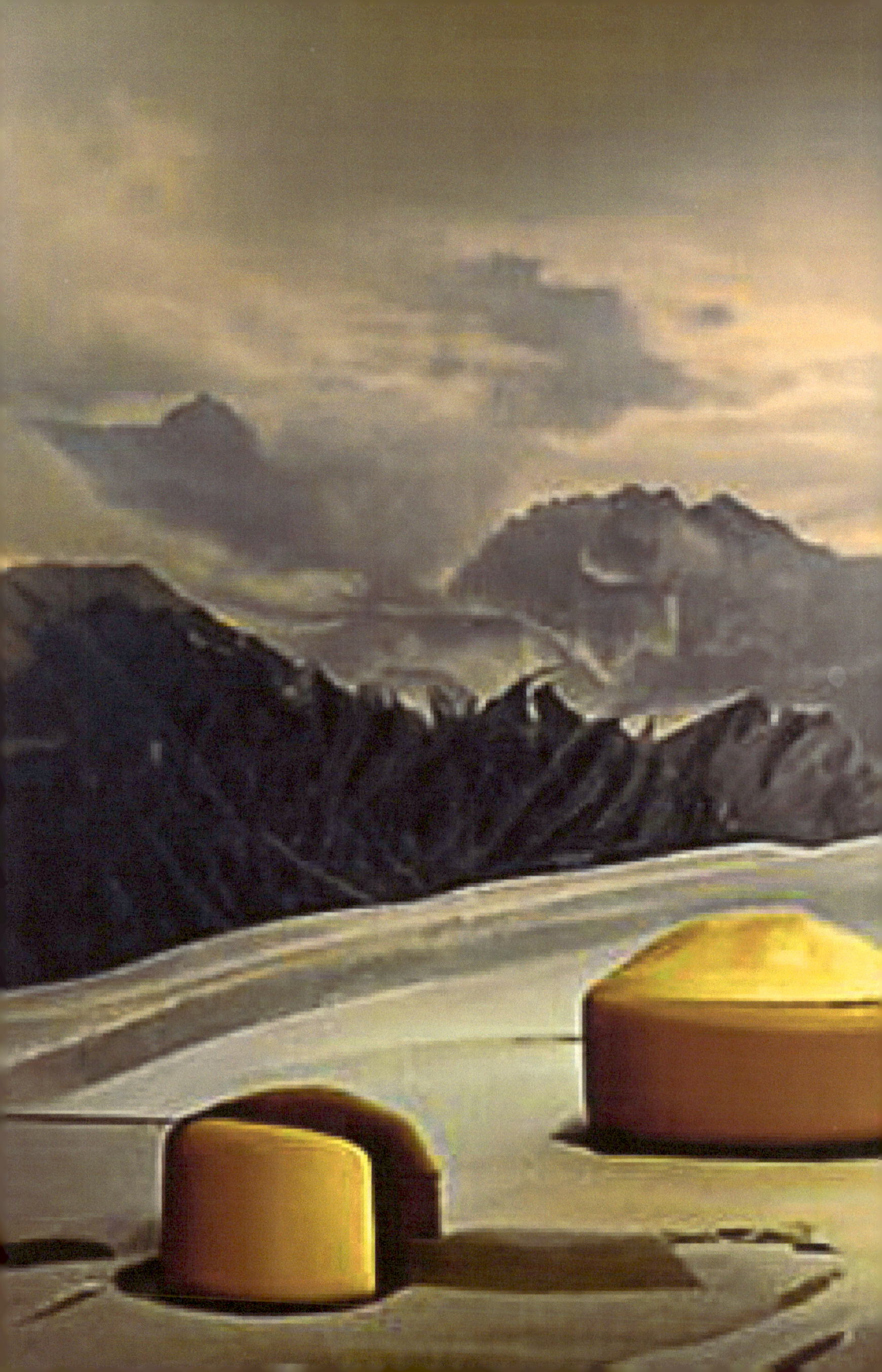

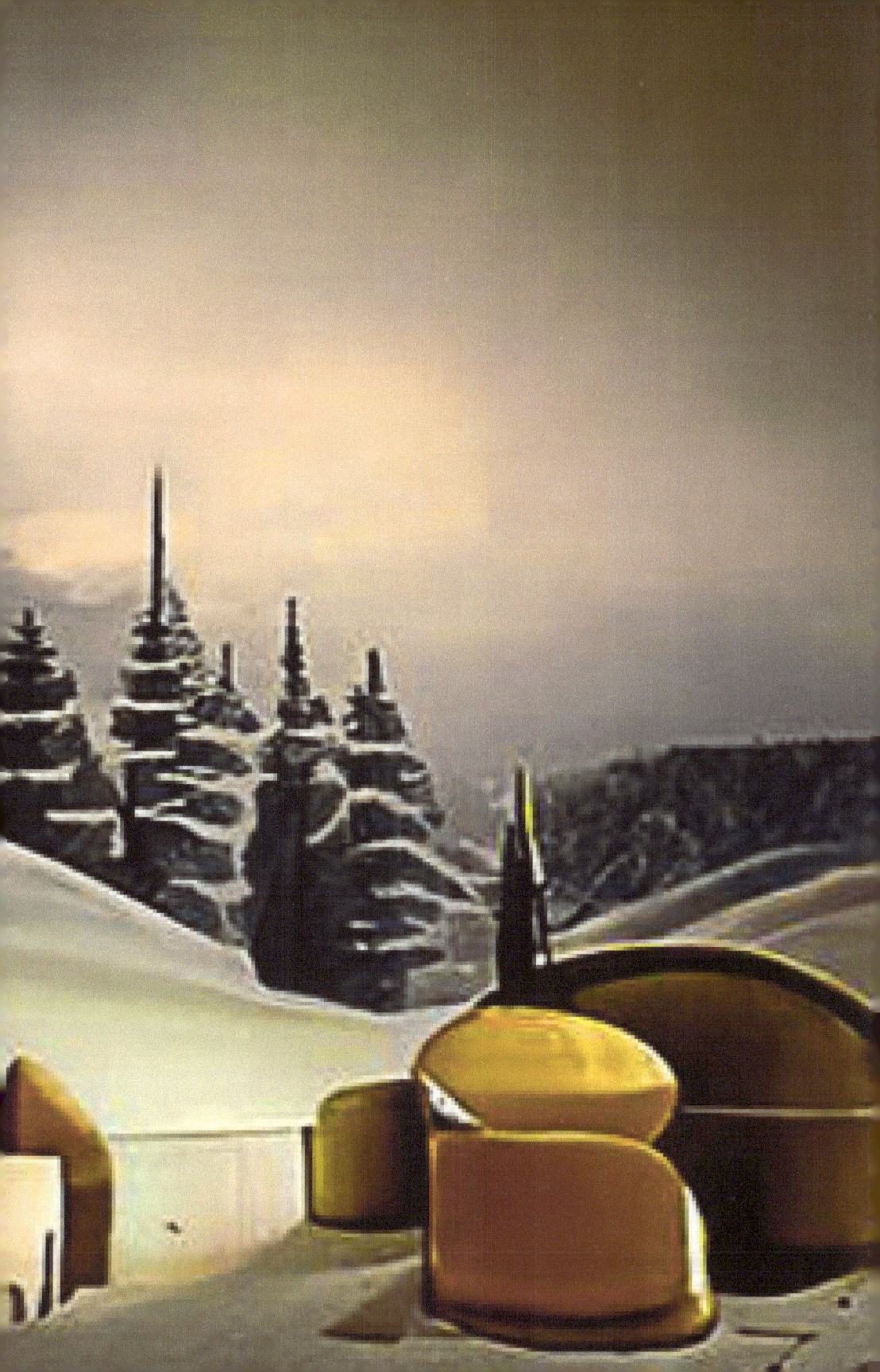

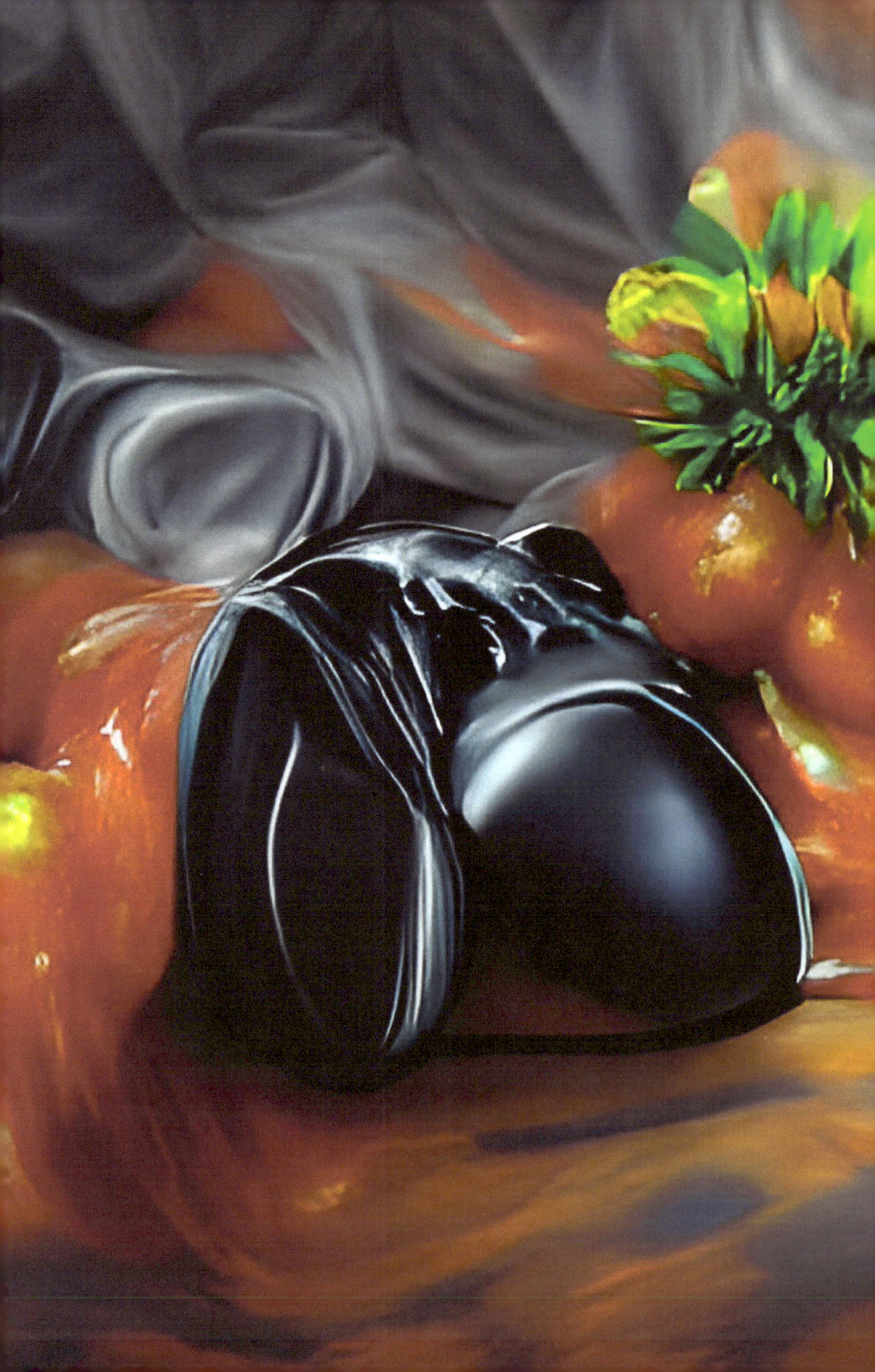

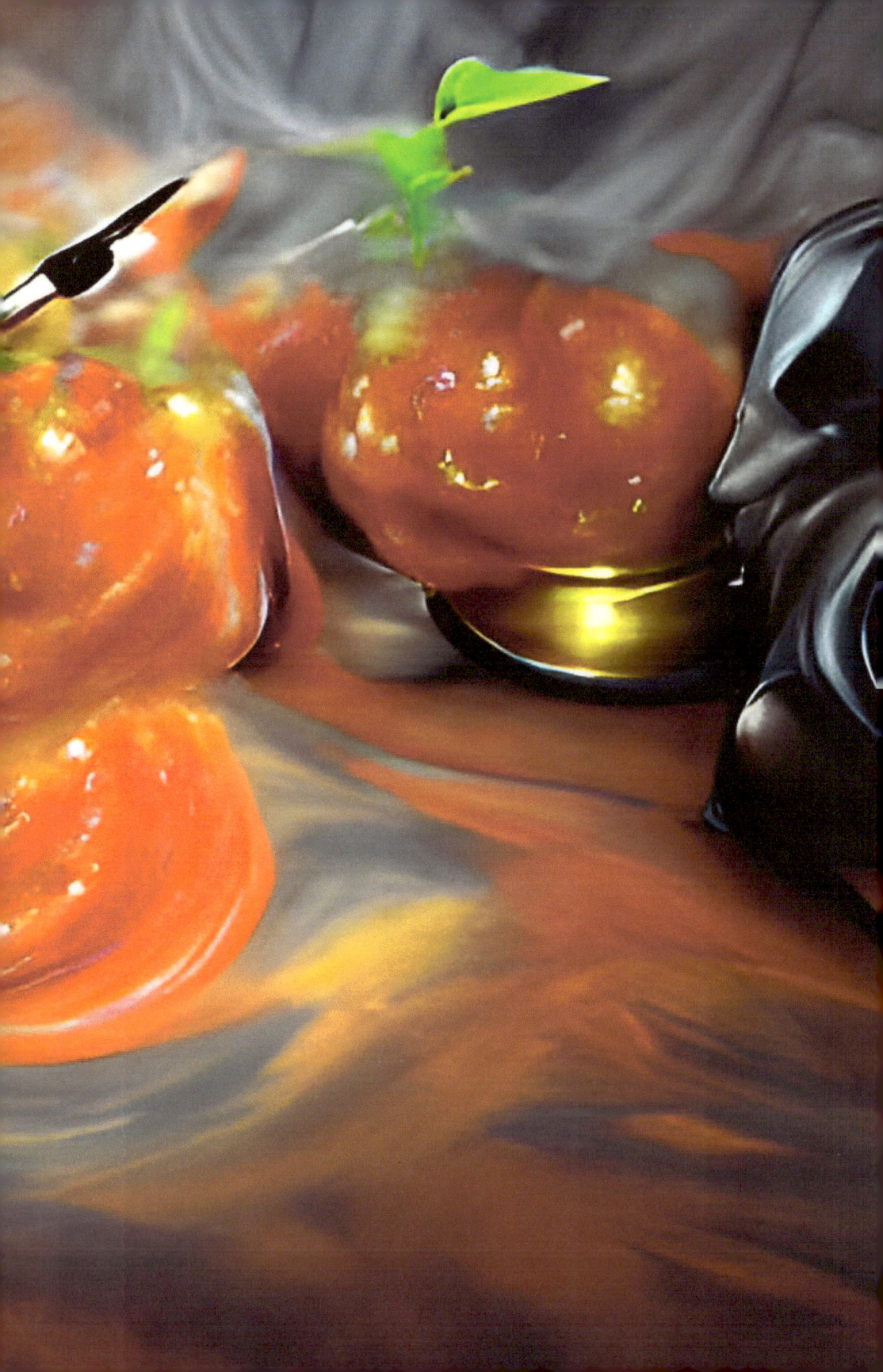

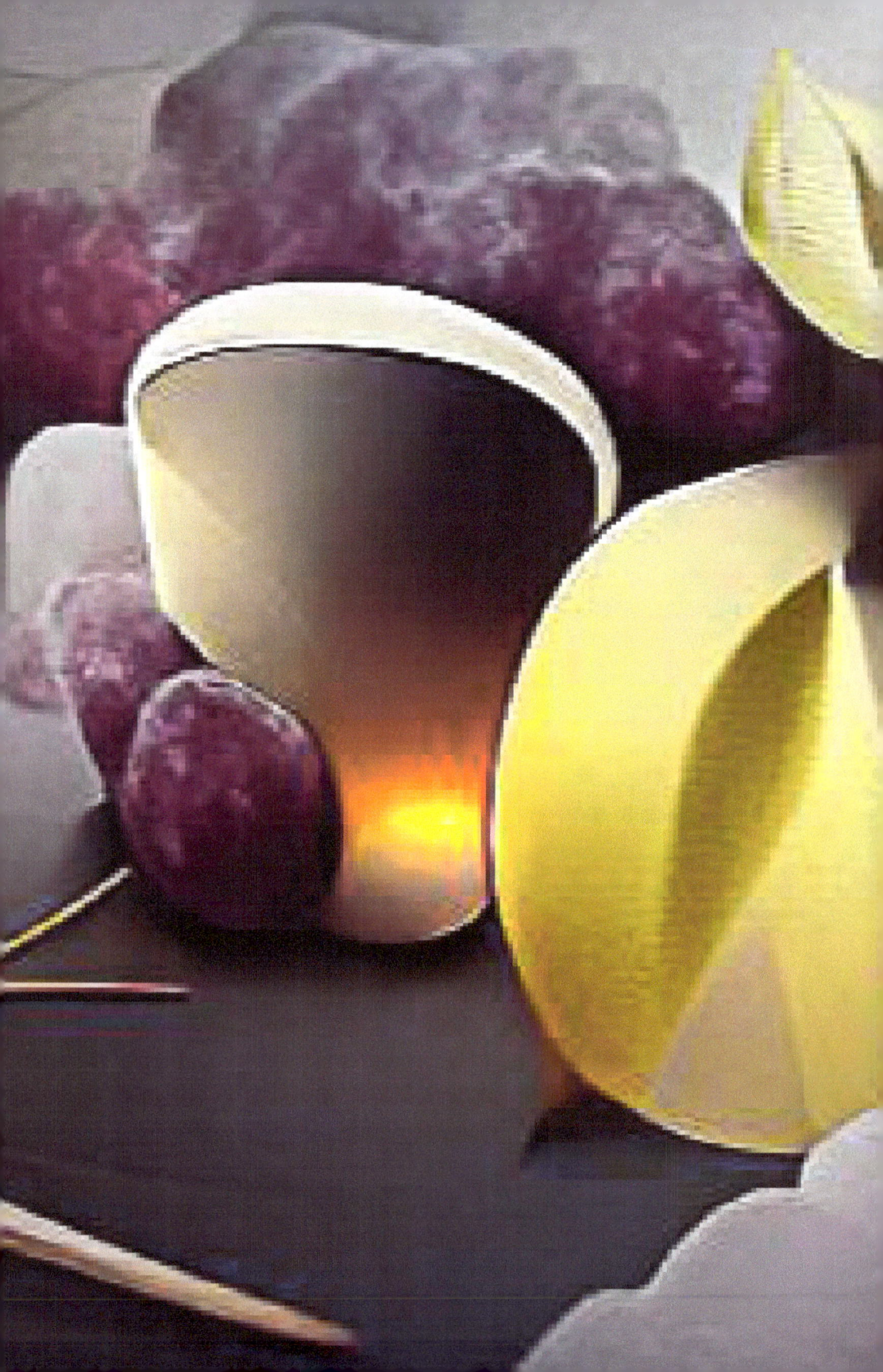

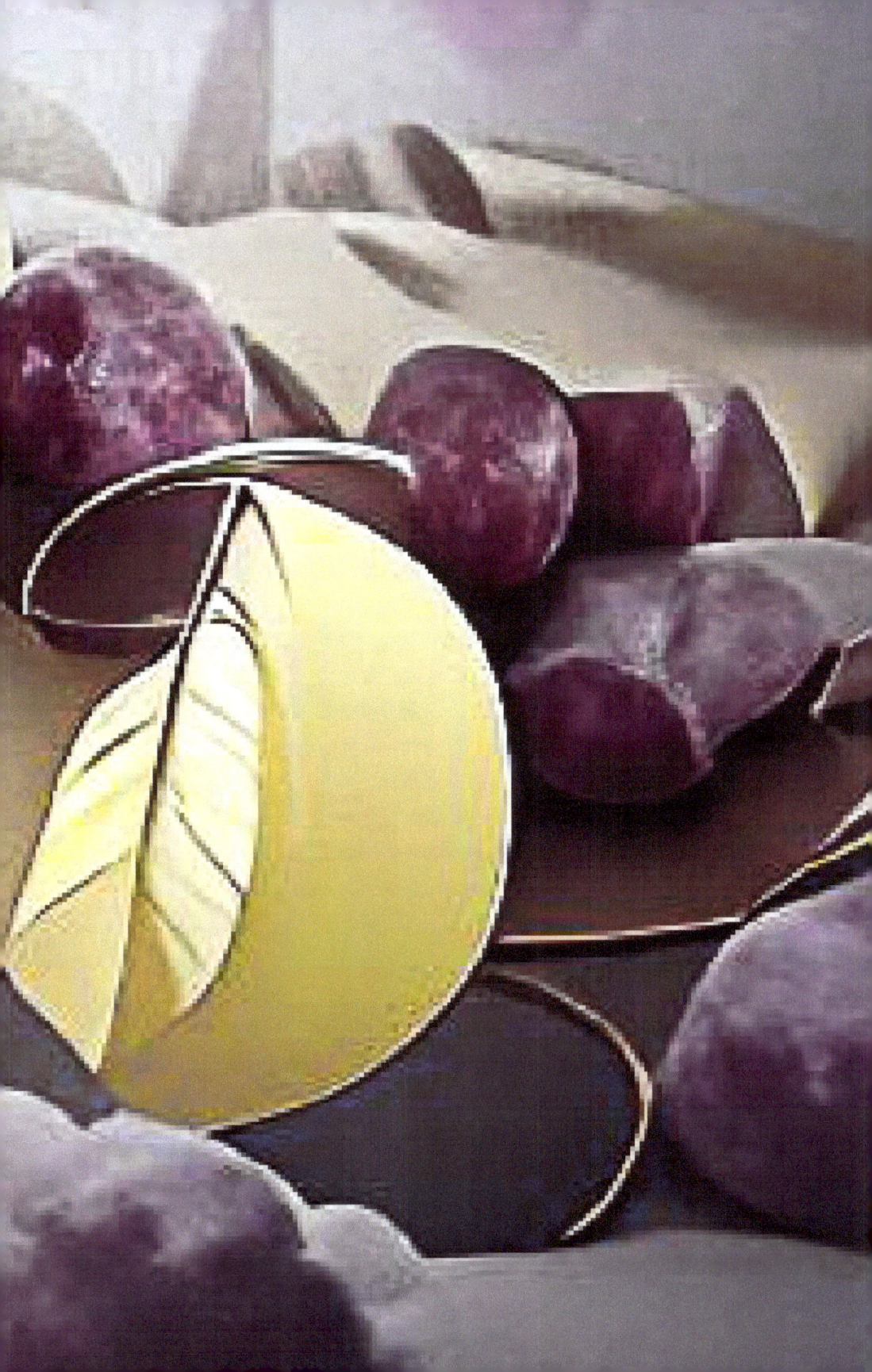

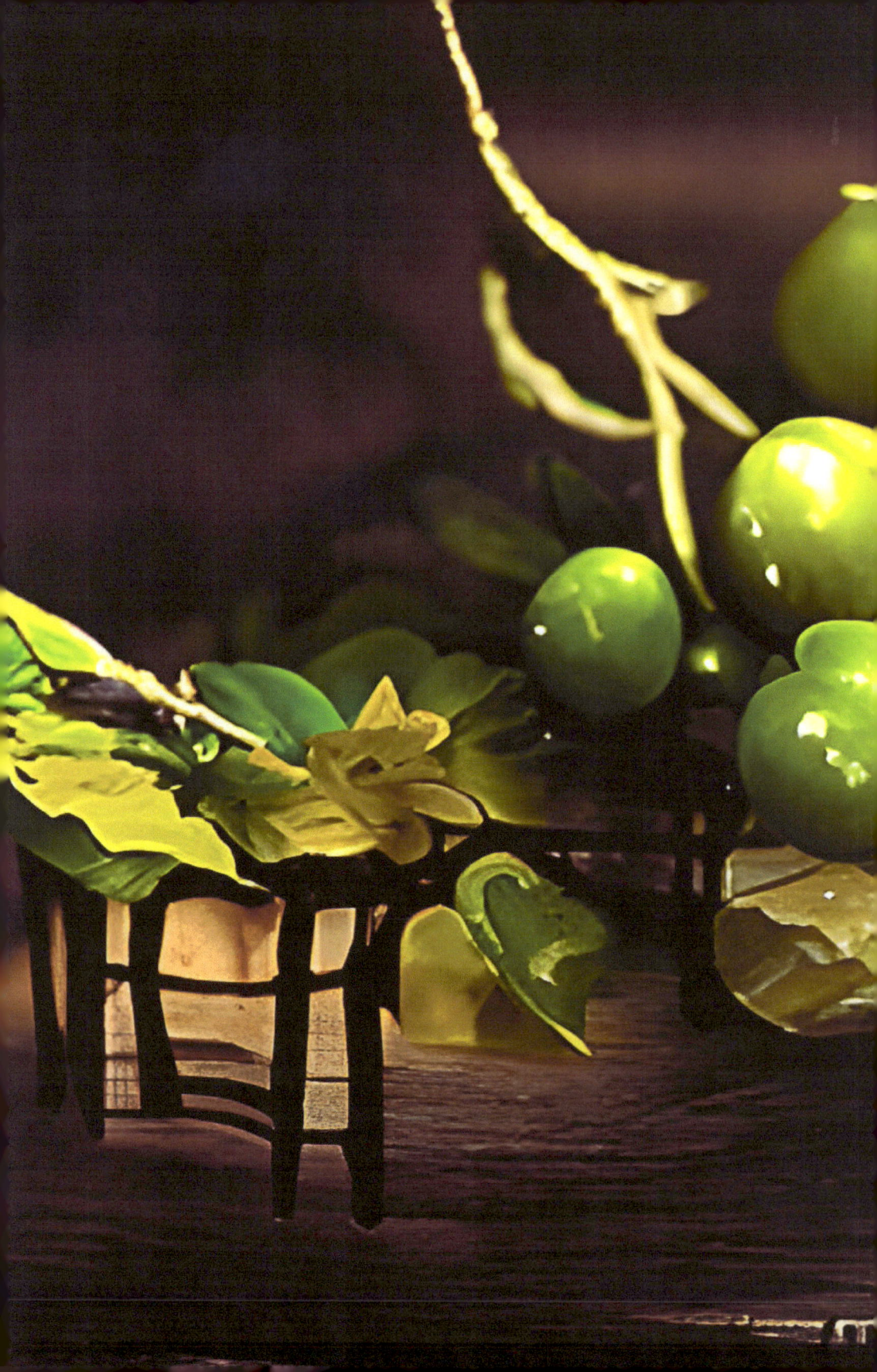

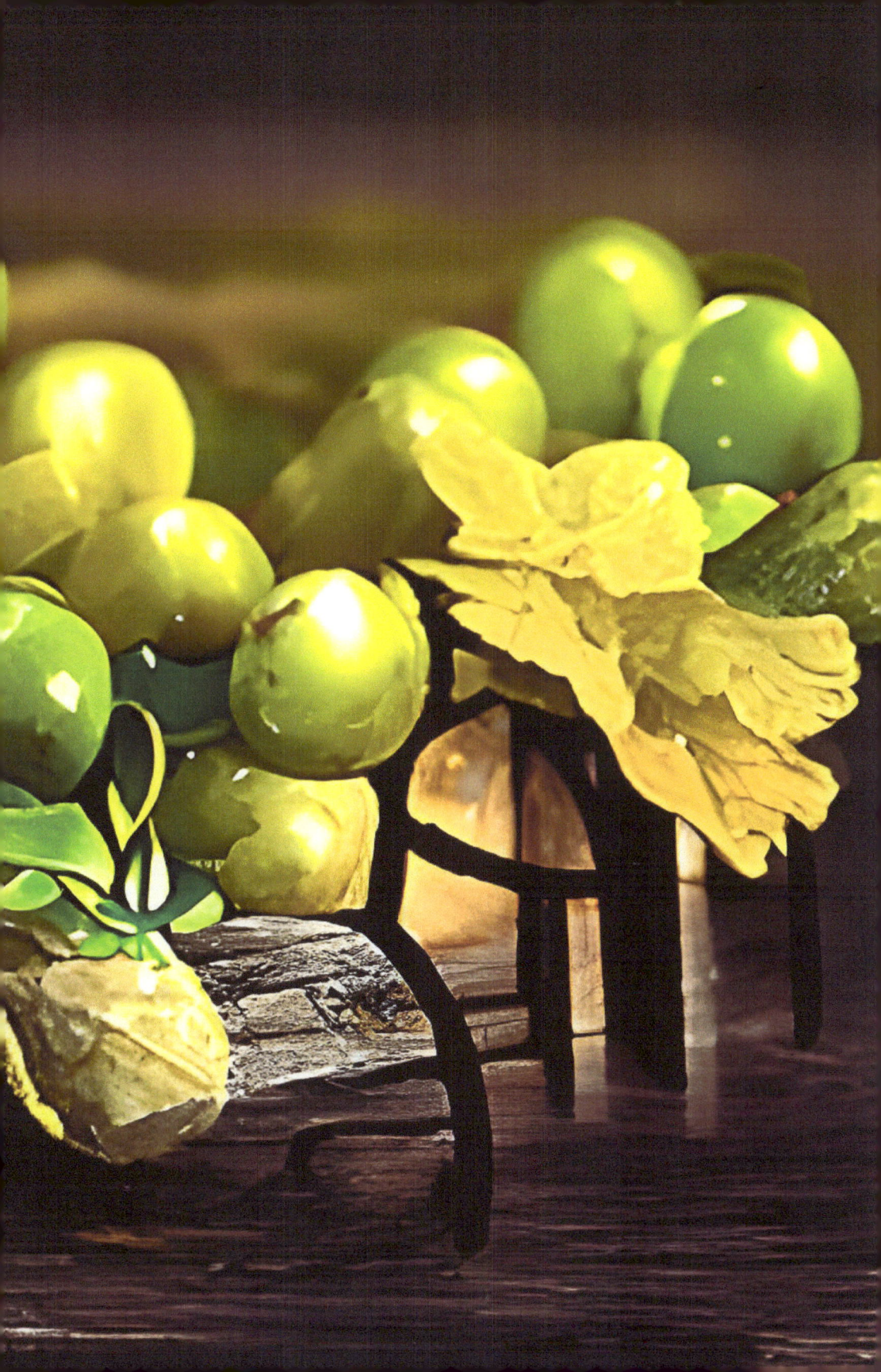

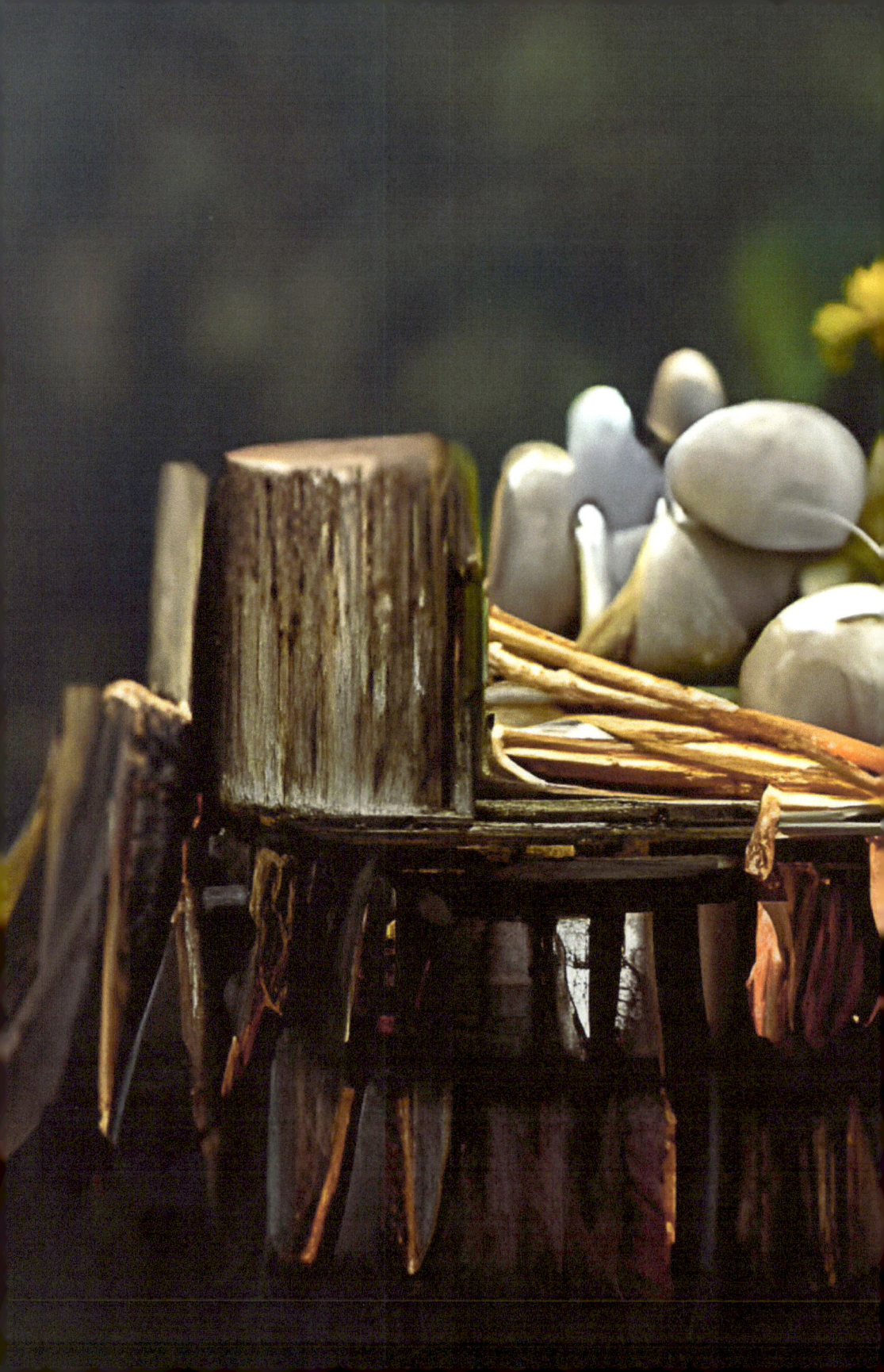

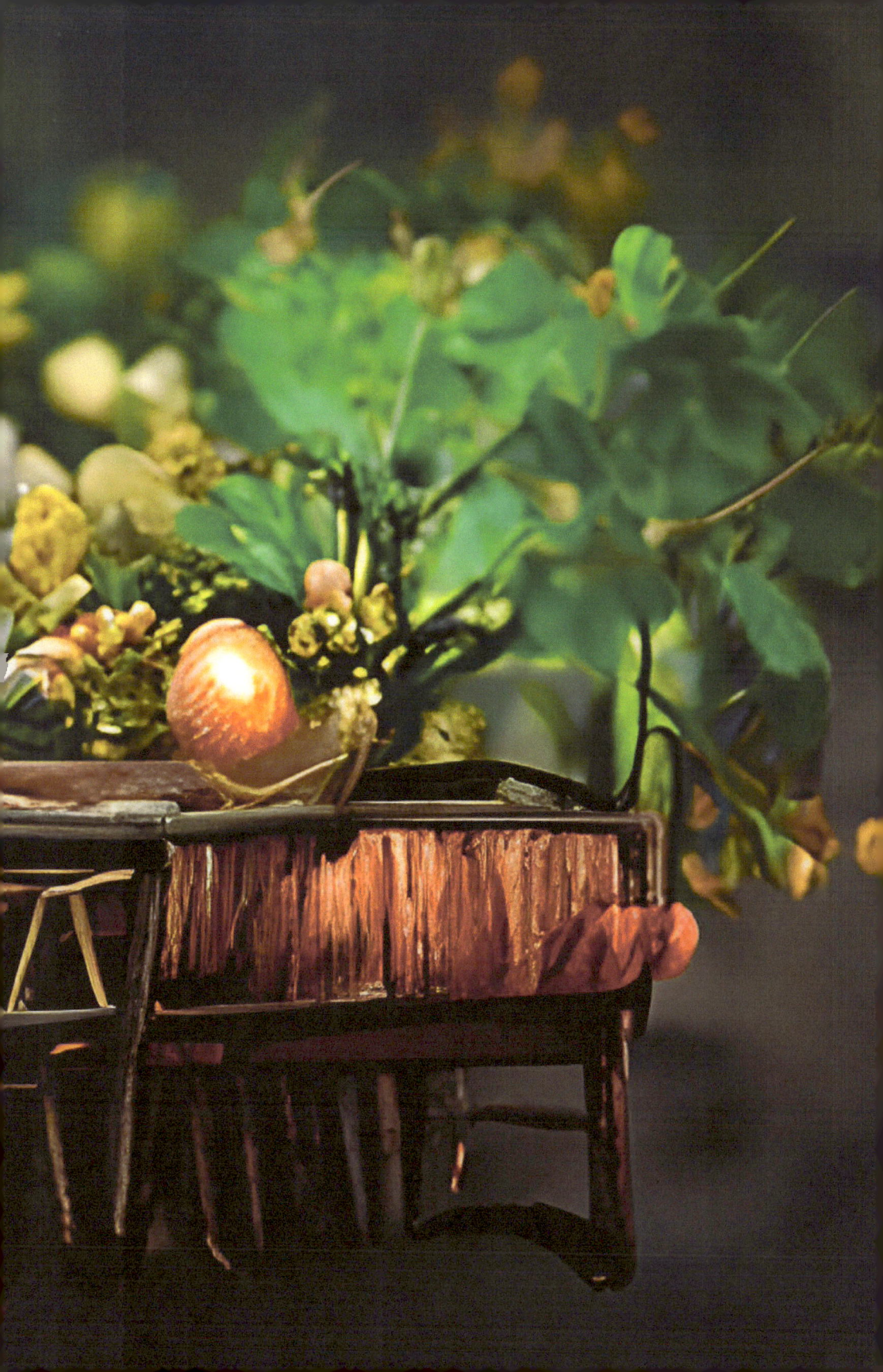

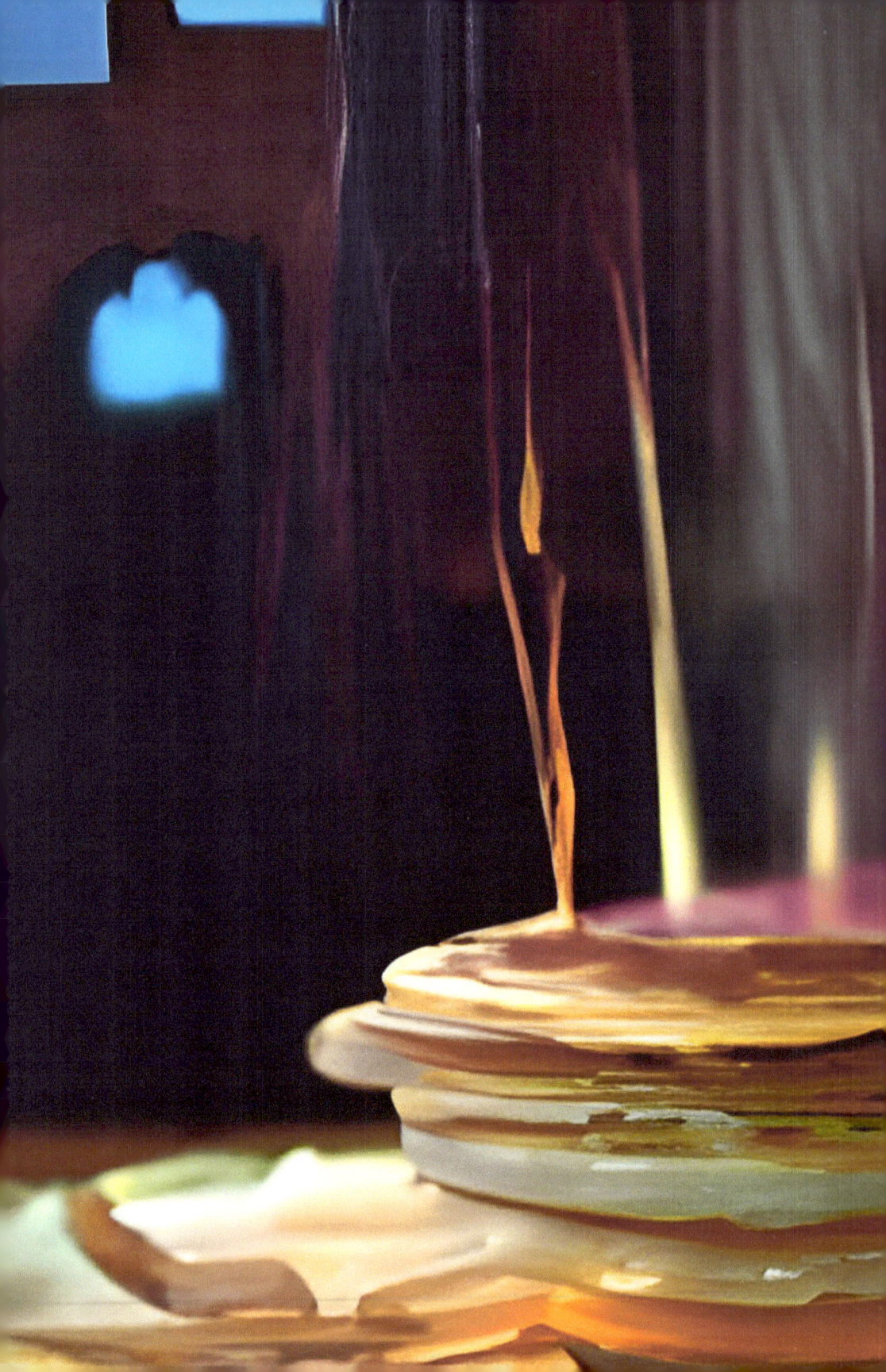

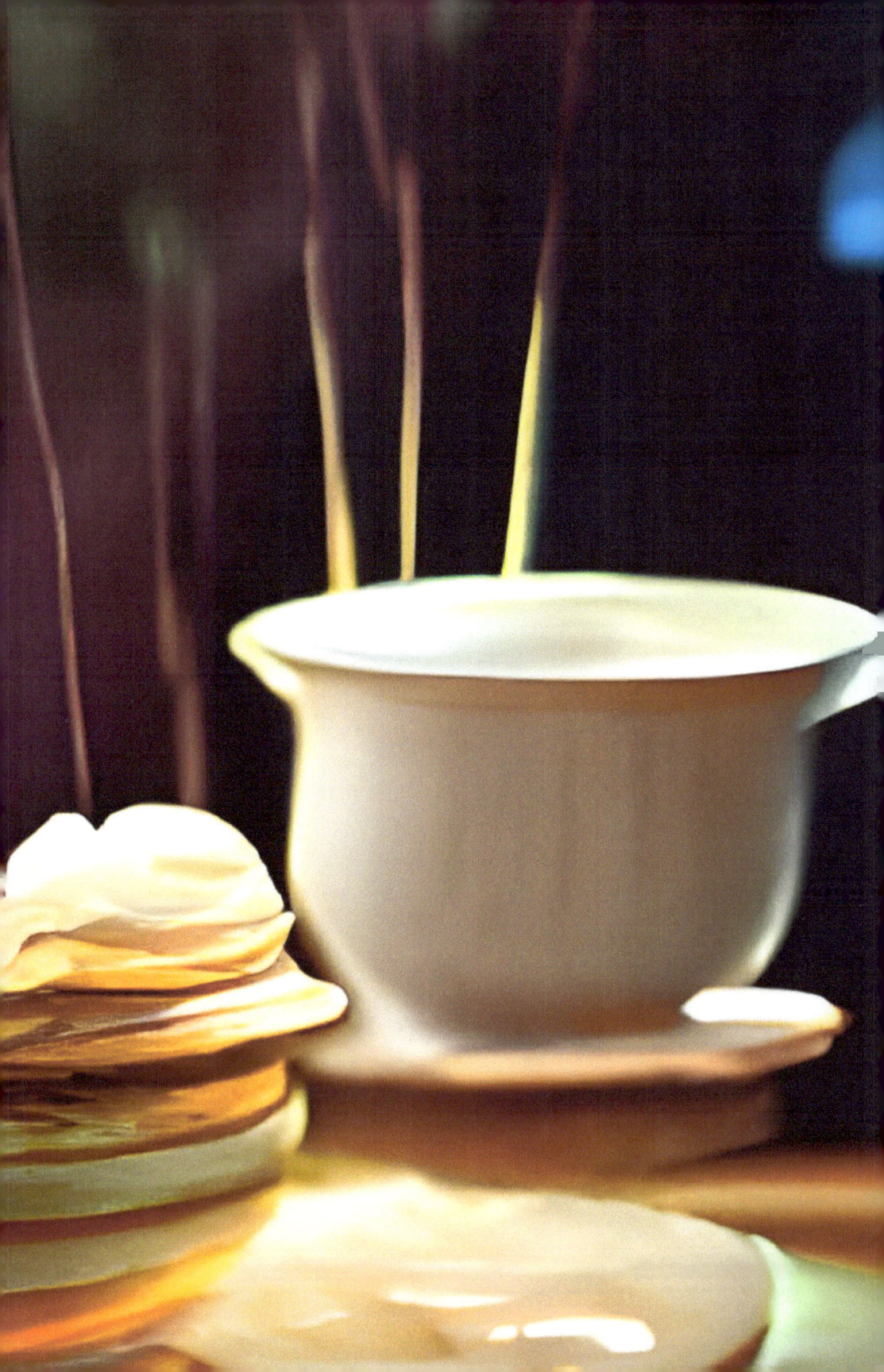

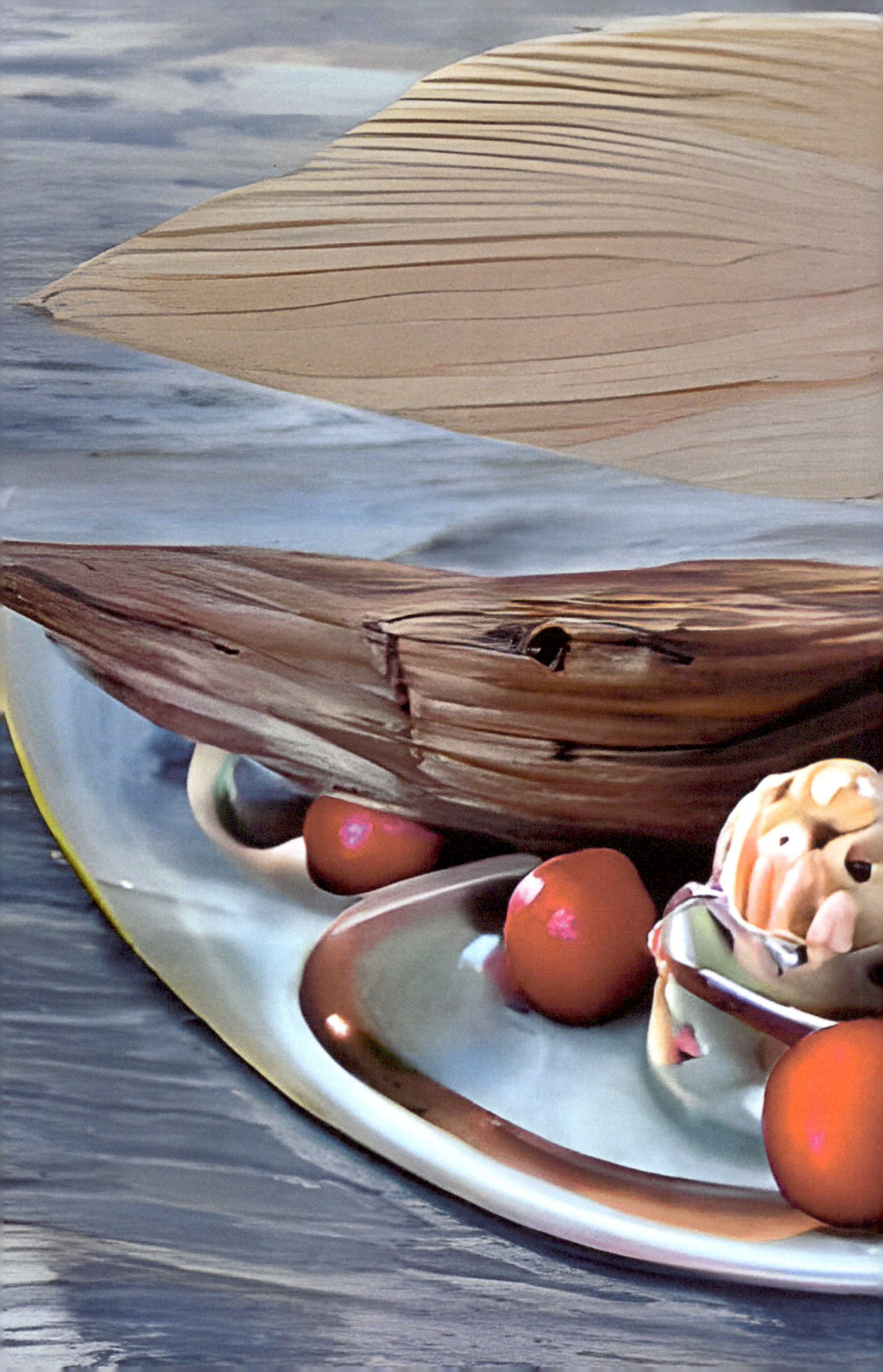

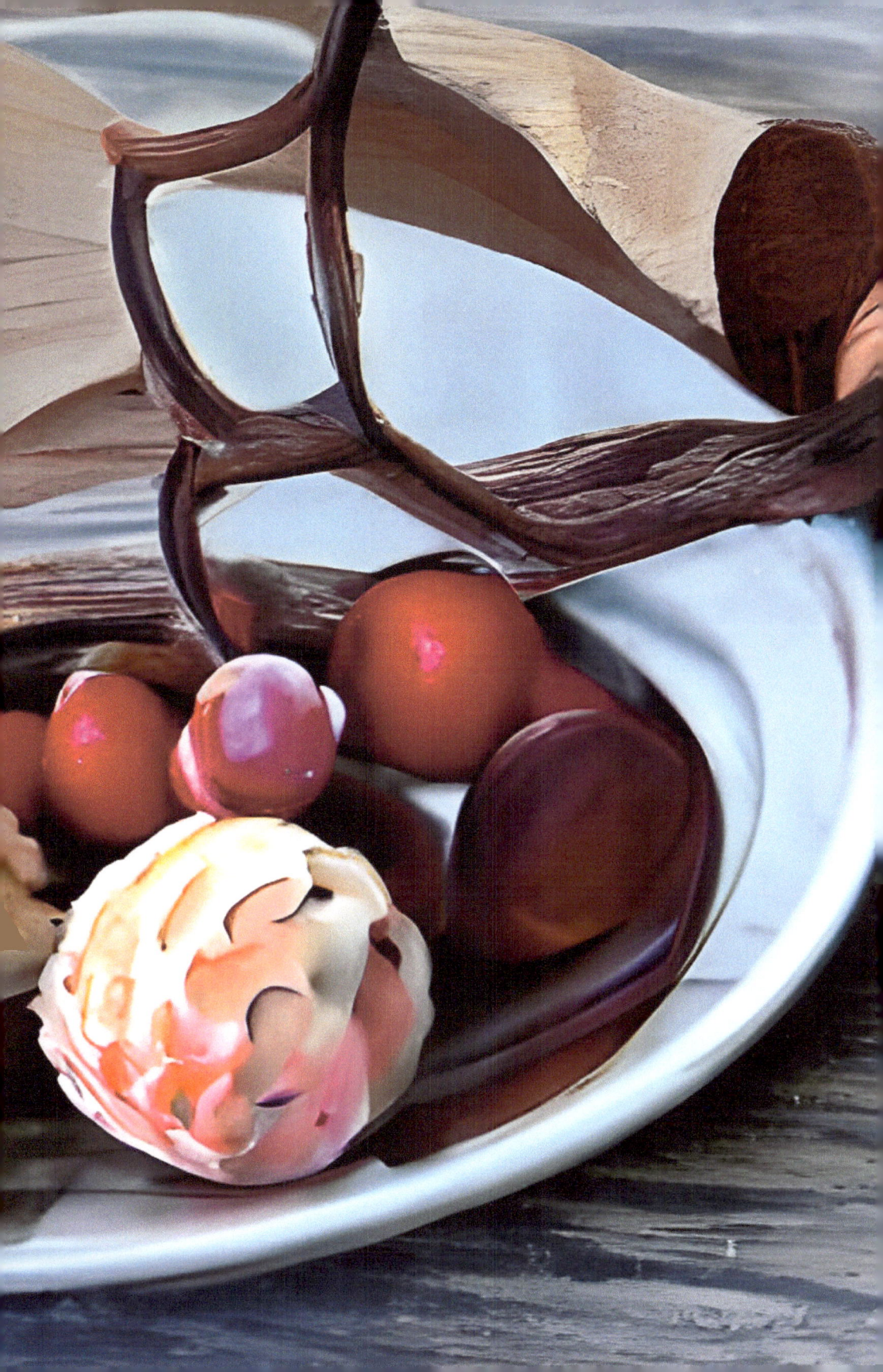

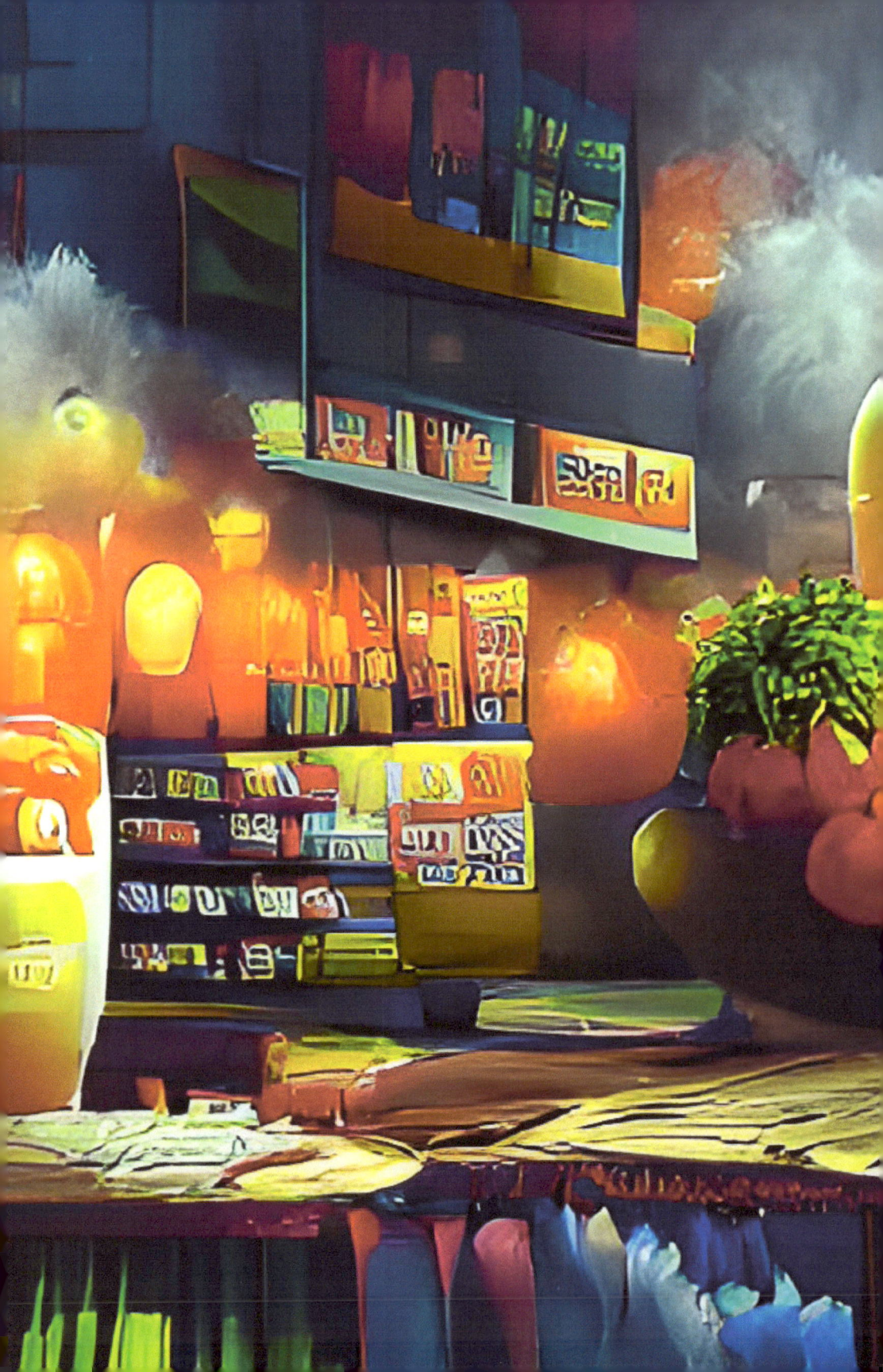

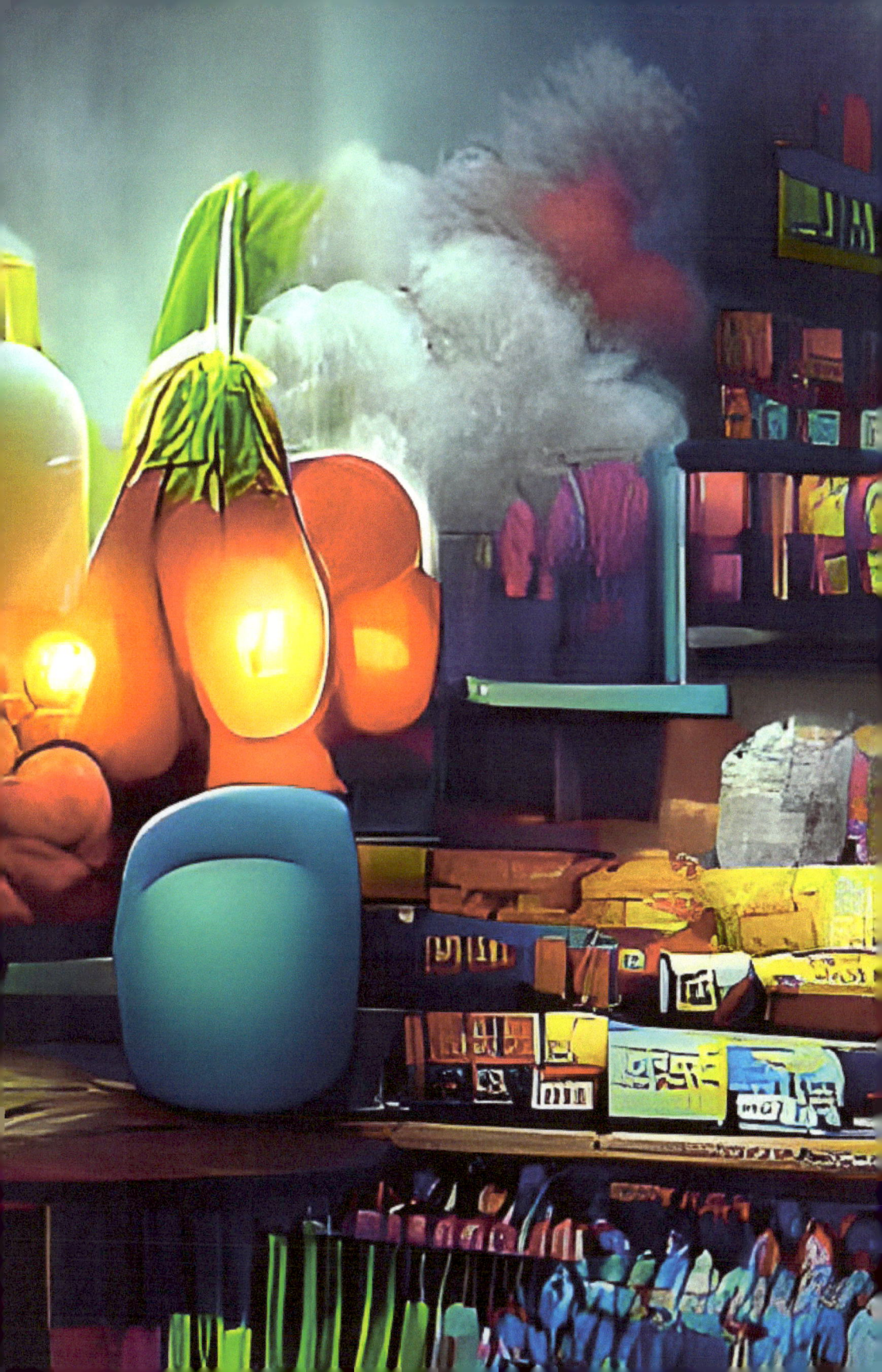

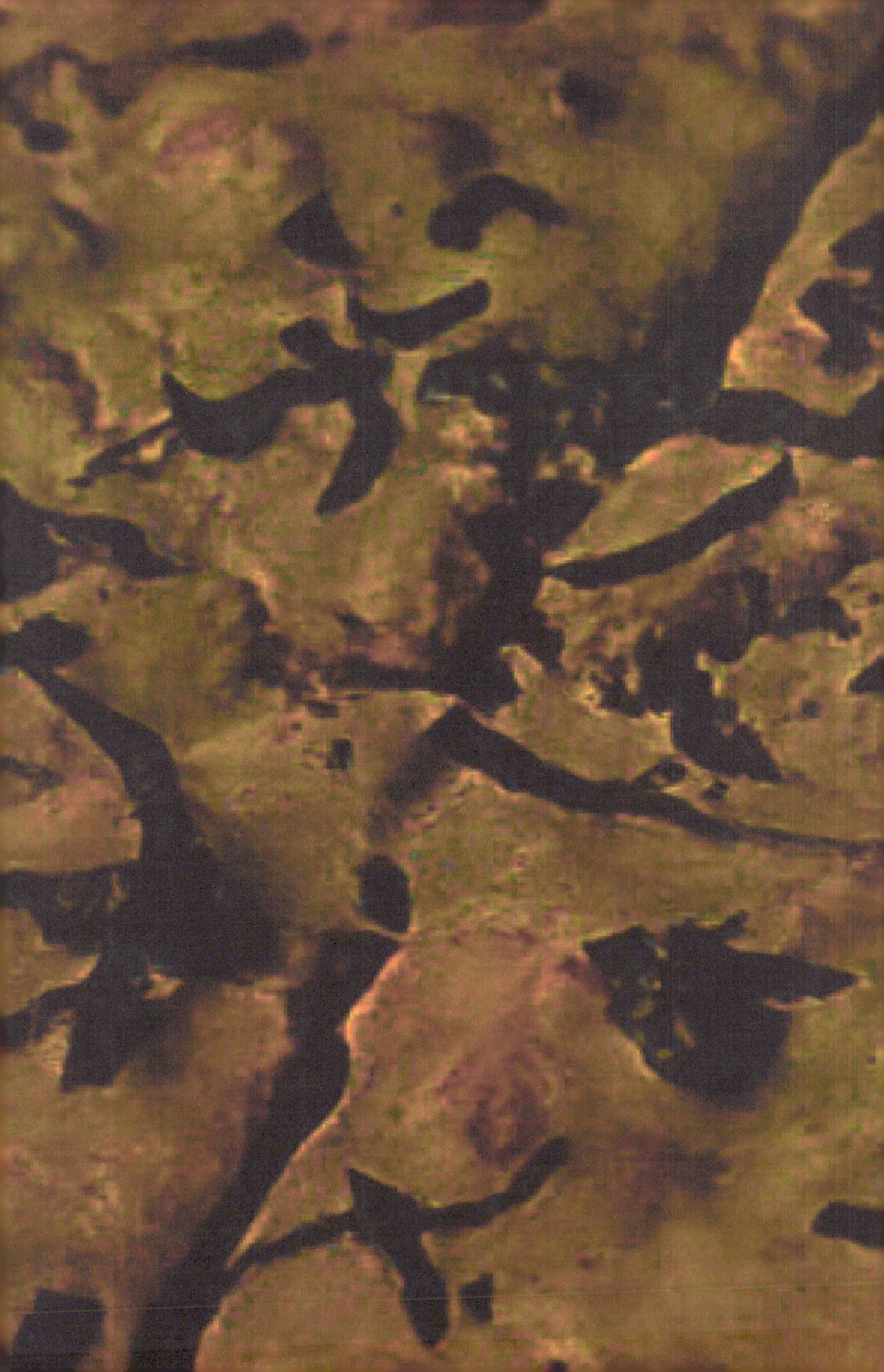

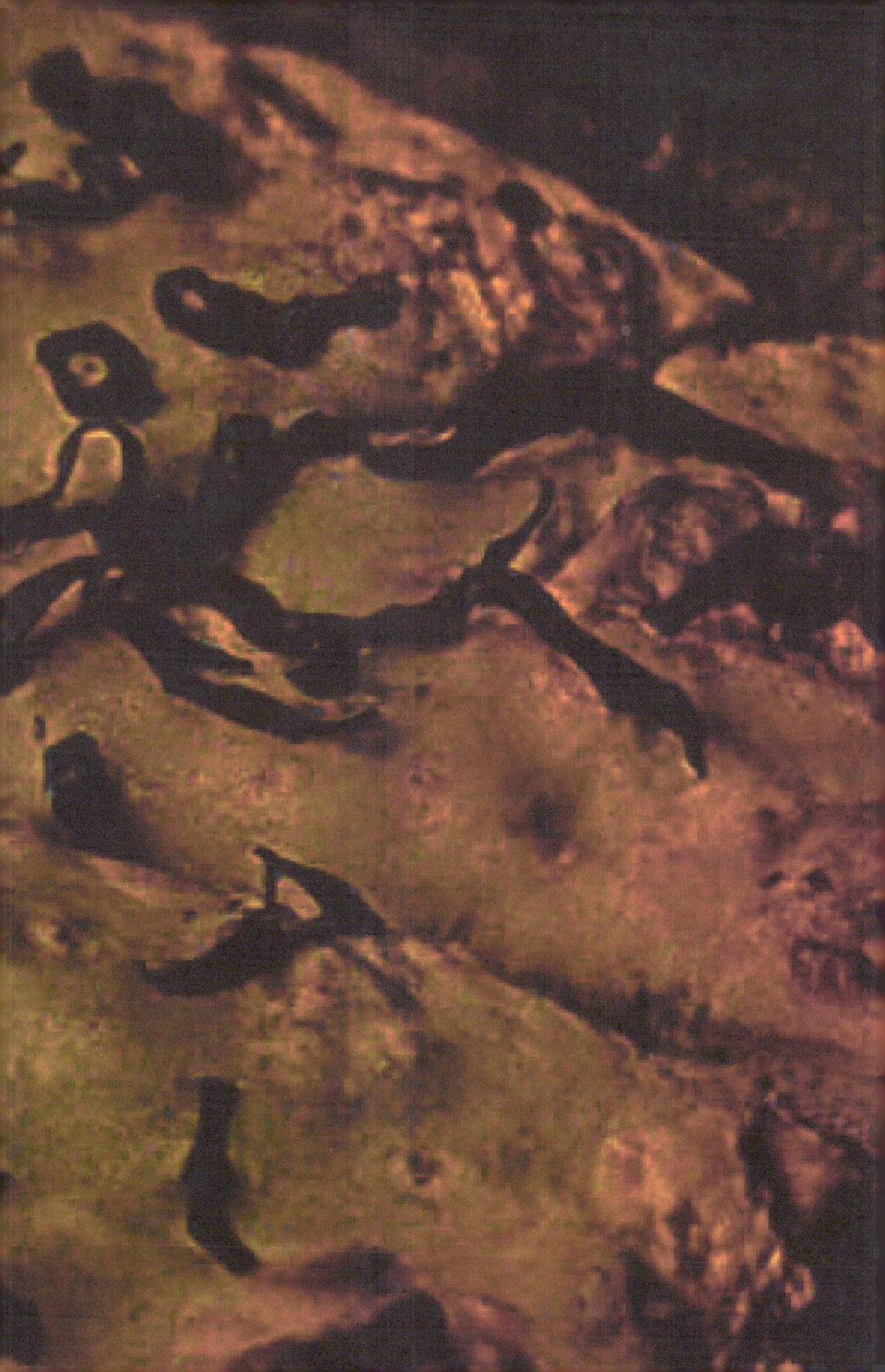

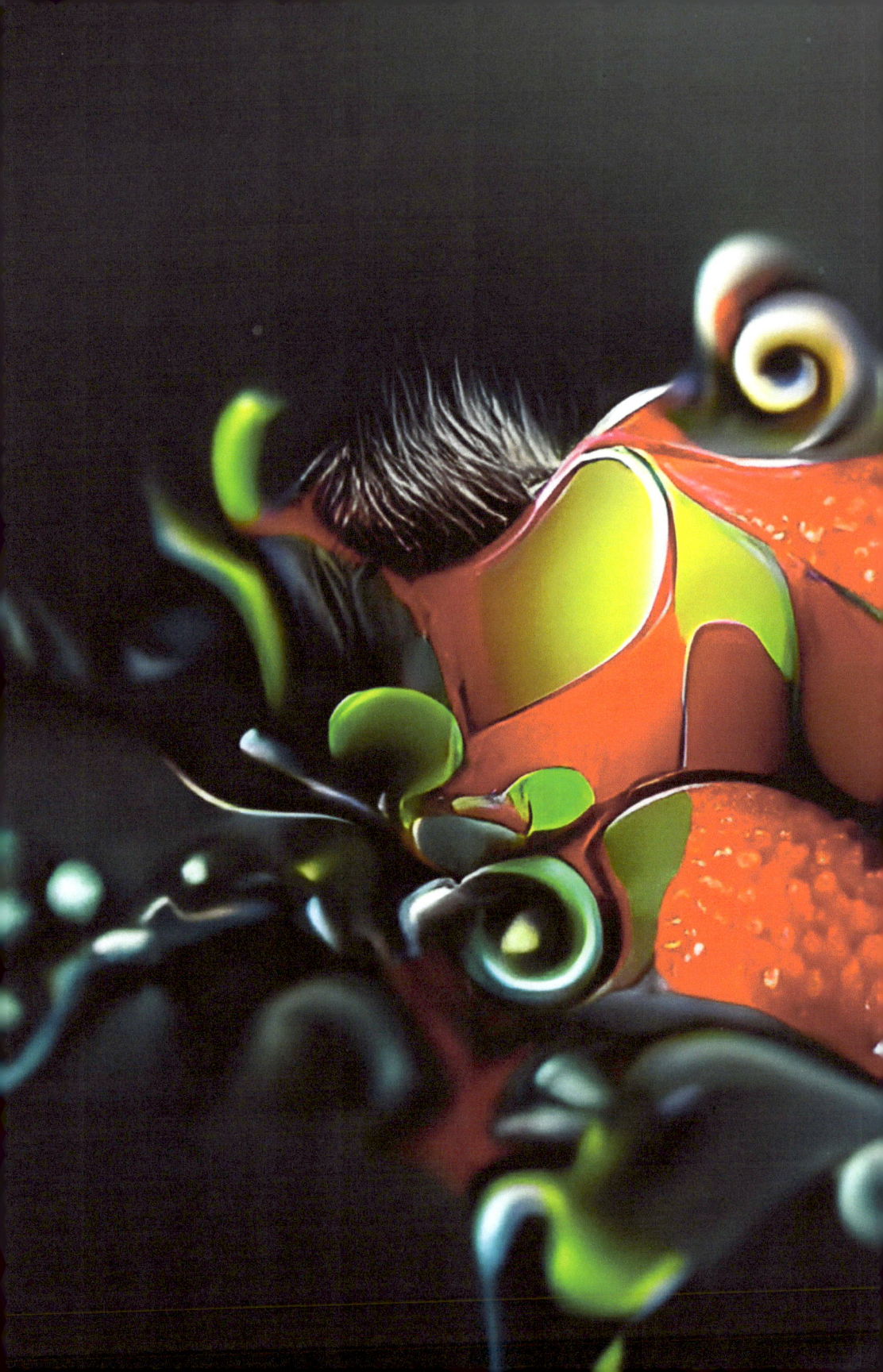

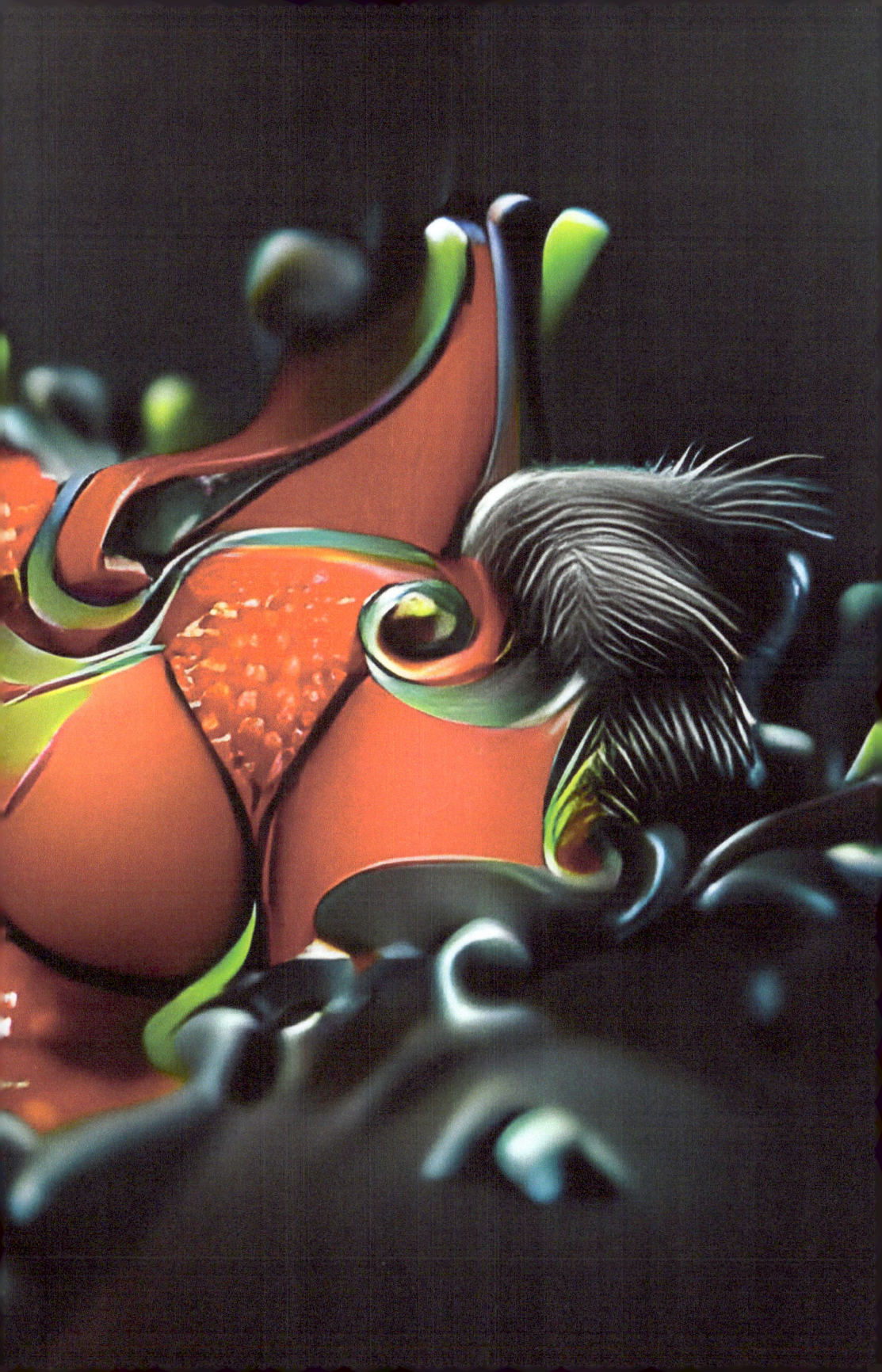

The End

I'm very pleased to invite you to my next Artbook

Thanks for your support!

Silvia F.R.

Contact info:

ateliercanaldigital@gmail.com

linktr.ee/atelierdigital

www.ingramcontent.com/pod-product-compliance
Lightning Source LLC
Chambersburg PA
CBHW040330220526
45473CB00009B/2638